THE CREST-JEWEL OF WISDOM

(VIVEKACHUDAMANI)

and other writings of

SANKARACHARYA

Translation and Commentary

by

CHARLES JOHNSTON

Typesetting © 2012 The Freedom Religion Press

www.thefreedomreligionpress.com

www.seeseer.com

ISBN: 978-1-937995-99-7

CONTENTS

INTRODUCTORY

by

CHARLES JOHNSTON

SANKARA, THE TEACHER

*The Upanishads, Buddha, and Sankara: these are the
three great lights of Indian wisdom. The Upanishads far
away in the golden age; in the bright dawn that has faded so
many ages ago. Buddha, the Awakened One, who,
catching in his clear spirit the glow of that early dawn,
sought to reflect it in the hearts of all men, of whatever race,
of whatever nation; sought to break down the barriers of
caste and priestly privilege; to leave each man alone with the
Universe, with no mediator between. But scattering abroad
the rays of wisdom, Buddha found that the genius of each
man, of each race, could only reflect one little beam;
and that in thus making the light the property of all men,
the purity and completeness of the light might be impaired.*

*Then followed Sankaracharya – Sankara the Teacher
– who set himself to the preservation of the light;
to burnishing the casket that held the lamp of wisdom.
Busying himself chiefly with India, he saw that the light must
be preserved, as far as its completeness and perfection were
concerned, within the Brahman order, where the advantages
of heredity, of ages of high ideals and rigid discipline could
best secure the purity of the light; could best supply a body of
men, fitted by character and training to master the high
knowledge, to sustain the moral effort that made the glory of
India's Golden age.*

This task of fitting the Brahman order to carry the torch of wisdom was undertaken by Sankara the Teacher in three ways. First, by commenting on the Great Upanishads and the Bhagavad Gita, he rendered the knowledge of the Golden Age into the thought and language of the Brahmans of his day. Second, by writing a series of preparatory works, of catechisms and manuals, he made smooth the path of those who would take the first steps on the path of wisdom. Thirdly, by a system of reform and discipline within the Brahman order, he did all that sound practice could do to second clear precept.

The system formed by Sankara within the Brahman order largely continues at the present day. The radiant points of this system are the monasteries founded by the Teacher, where a succession of teachers, each initiated by his predecessor, carry on the spiritual tradition of the great Sankara unbroken.

Of commentaries on the Upanishads and the Bhagavad Gita, many, perhaps, were written in a gradual series leading up from simple truths to the more profound mysteries; so that, with one after another of these treatises in hand, the learner was gradually led to the heart of the mystery which lies "like a germ of generation" well concealed in these matchless theosophic documents. These commentaries were followed by others, the work of Sankara's pupils; and though these works of explanation are very numerous, all those that are published seem to belong to the earlier states of learning, and leave the deeper passages and problems of the Upanishads still unsolved.

But the other part of Sankara's work, the manuals and catechisms for learners, are complete and perfect. They really teach, quite plainly and lucidly, the first steps on the path of wisdom; they point out, with clear insistence, the qualities that are necessary to make these first steps fruitful; qualities without which the learner may remain, hesitating and halting, on the threshold, through lack of the force and sterling moral worth which alone make any further progress possible.

Nor are these necessary qualities difficult to understand. They are not queer psychic powers that only flatter vanity; they are not mere intellectual tricks that leave the heart cold; they are rather the simple qualities of sterling honesty, of freedom from selfishness and sensuality – which have formed the basis of every moral code; the virtues so common and commonplace on the lips, but not quite so common in the life and character.

These treatises of Sankara speak to the common understanding and moral sense in an unparalleled degree. They are an appeal to the reason that has hardly ever been equaled for clearness and simplicity by the sages of the earth. Their aim is Freedom (Moksha), "Freedom from the bondage of the world." This aim speaks to every one, awakens an echo in every heart, appeals to the universal hope of common humanity.

But it is not enough for the mind to follow the lucid sentences of Sankara. "Freedom from the bondage of the world" demands something more. "Sickness is not cured by saying 'Medicine,' but by drinking it; so a man is not set free by the name of the Eternal, but by discerning the Eternal." The teaching must be woven into life and character if it is to bear fruit; it is not enough to contemplate the virtue of freedom from selfishness and sensuality in the abstract.

One of these treatises, "The Crest-Jewel of Wisdom," will be translated here. It will be divided according to the natural sections of the text, beginning with the first steps on the path and ending with the complete teaching of Sankara's philosophy so far as that teaching can be put into words. Hardly any notes will be necessary, as the language of the teacher is lucidity itself. Every word is defined and every definition enlarged and repeated.

It is not, however, the object of these papers to put forward a presentation of eastern thought merely to be read and forgotten. We shall spare no pains of repetition and amplification to make the thoughts of the East quite clear. But much remains to be done by readers themselves. They must make the thoughts of Sankara and the sages their own spiritual property if they are to benefit by them, and as a preliminary for this first chapter of Sankara's teaching, the "four Perfections" should be learned by heart and taken to heart.

THE CREST-JEWEL OF WISDOM

(VIVEKACHUDAMANI)

FIRST STEPS ON THE PATH

PROLOGUE

(VERSES 1 – 15)

I bow before Govinda,
the objectless object of final success in the highest wisdom,
who is supreme bliss and the true teacher.

For beings a human birth is hard to win, then manhood
and holiness, then excellence in the path of wise law;
hardest of all to win is wisdom. Discernment between Self
and not-Self, true judgment, nearness to the Self of the
Eternal and Freedom are not gained without a myriad of right
acts in a hundred births. This triad that is won by the bright
one's favor is hard to gain: humanity, aspiration, and rest in
the great spirit. After gaining at last a human birth,
hard to win, then manhood and knowledge of the teaching,
if one strives not after Freedom he is a fool.
He, suicidal, destroys himself by grasping after the unreal.
Who is more self-deluded than he who is careless of his own
welfare after gaining a hard-won human birth and manhood,
too? Let them declare the laws, let them offer to the gods,
let them perform all rites, let them love the gods;
without knowing the oneness with the Self,
Freedom is not won even in a hundred years of the Evolver.
"There is no hope of immortality through riches,"
says the scripture.
It is clear from this that rites cannot lead to Freedom.

Therefore let the wise one strive after Freedom,
giving up all longing for sensual self-indulgence;
approaching the good, great Teacher (the Higher Self),
with soul intent on the object of the teaching.

8

Let him by the Self raise the Self, sunk in the ocean of the world, following the path of union through complete recognition of oneness. Setting all rites aside, let the wise, learned ones who approach the study of the Self strive for Freedom from the bondage of the world.
Rites are to purify the thoughts, but not to gain the reality. The real is gained by Wisdom, not by a myriad of rites.
When one steadily examines and clearly sees a rope, the fear that it is a serpent is destroyed. Knowledge is gained by discernment, by examining, by instruction, but not by bathing, nor gifts, nor a hundred holdings of the breath.
Success demands first ripeness;
questions of time and place are subsidiary.
Let the seeker after self-knowledge find the Teacher (the Higher Self), full of kindness and knowledge of the Eternal.

THE FOUR PERFECTIONS

(Verses 16 – 34)

He is ripe to seek the Self
who is full of knowledge and wisdom, reason and discernment, and who bears the well-known marks.

He is ready to seek the Eternal who has Discernment and Dispassion; who has Restfulness and the other graces.

Four perfections are numbered by the wise.
When they are present there is success,
but in their absence there is failure.

First is counted
the Discernment between things lasting and unlasting.
Next Dispassion,
the indifference to self-indulgence here and in paradise.
Then the Six Graces, beginning with Restfulness.
Then the longing for Freedom.

A certainty like this
– the Eternal is real, the fleeting world is unreal –
this is that Discernment between things lasting and unlasting.

9

And this is Dispassion –
a perpetual willingness to give up all sensual self-indulgence –
everything lower than the Eternal,
through a constant sense of their insufficiency.

Then the Six Graces:
a steady intentness of the mind on its goal; this is Restfulness.

And the steadying of the powers that act and perceive,
each in its own sphere, turning them back from sensuality –
this is Self control.

Then the raising of the mind above external things –
this is the true Withdrawal.

The enduring of all ills without petulance
and without self-pity – this is right Endurance.

An honest confidence in the teaching and the Teacher –
this is that Faith by which the treasure is gained.

The intentness of the soul on the pure Eternal –
this is right Meditation, but not the indulgence of fancy.

The wish to untie, by discernment of their true nature,
all the bonds woven by unwisdom, the bonds of selfishness
and sensuality – this is the longing for Freedom.

Though at first imperfect, these qualities gradually
growing through Dispassion, Restfulness, and the other graces
and the Teacher's help will gain their due.

When Dispassion and the longing for Freedom are
strong, then Restfulness and the other graces will bear fruit.

But when these two –
Dispassion and the longing for Freedom – are lacking,
then Restfulness and the other graces are a mere appearance,
like water in the desert (a mirage.)

Chief among the causes of Freedom is devotion,
the intentness of the soul on its own nature.
Or devotion may be called intentness on the reality of the Self.

Let him who possesses these Perfections and who
would learn the reality of the Self, approach the wise Teacher
(the Higher Self), from whom comes the loosing of bonds;
who is full of knowledge and perfect; who is not beaten by
desire, who really knows the Eternal; who has found rest in
the Eternal, at peace like a fuelless fire; who is full of selfless
kindness, the friend of all that lives. Serving the Teacher with
devotion and aspiration for the Eternal, and finding harmony
with him, seek the needed knowledge of the Self.

THE APPEAL TO THE HIGHER SELF

(Verses 35 – 40)

"I submit myself to thee, Master,
friend of the bowed-down world
and river of selfless kindness."

"Raise me by thy guiding light
that pours forth the nectar of truth and mercy,
for I am sunk in the ocean of the world."

"I am burned by the hot flame of relentless life
and torn by the winds of misery:
save me from death, for I take refuge in thee,
finding no other rest."

The great good ones dwell in peace,
bringing joy to the world like the return of spring.
Having crossed the ocean of the world,
they ever help others to cross over.

For this is the very nature
of the great-souled ones (Mahatmas) –
their swiftness to take away the weariness of others.
So the soft-rayed moon of itself soothes the earth,
burned by the fierce sun's heat.

"Sprinkle me with thy nectar voice
that brings the joy of eternal bliss, pure and cooling,
falling on me as from a cup, like the joy of inspiration;
for I am burnt by the hot, scorching flames of the world's fire."

"Happy are they on whom thy light rests,
even for a moment, and who reach harmony with thee."

"How shall I cross the ocean of the world?
Where is the path? What way must I follow? I know not,
Master. Save me from the wound of the world's pain."

THE BEGINNING OF THE TEACHING

(Verses 41 – 71)

To him, making this appeal and seeking help,
scorched by the flame of the world's fire, the Great Soul
beholding him with eyes most pitiful brings speedy comfort.

The Wise One instills the truth in him
who has approached him longing for Freedom,
who is following the true path,
calming the tumult of his mind and bringing Restfulness.

"Fear not, wise one, there is no danger for thee.
There is a way to cross over the ocean of the world,
and by this path the sages have reached the shore."

"This same path I point out to thee, for it is the way to
destroy the world's fear. Crossing the ocean of the world
by this path, thou shalt win the perfect joy."

By discerning the aim of the wisdom-teaching
(Vedanta) is born that most excellent knowledge.
Then comes the final ending of the world's pain. The voice of
the teaching plainly declares that faith, devotion, meditation,
and the search for union are the means of Freedom for him
who would be free. He who is perfect in these wins Freedom
from the bodily bondage woven by unwisdom.

When the Self is veiled by unwisdom
there arises a binding to the not-self,
and from this comes the pain of world-life. The fire of wisdom
lit by discernment between these two – Self and not-Self –
will wither up the source of unwisdom, root and all.

THE PUPIL ASKS

"Hear with selfless kindness, Master.
I ask this question:
receiving the answer from thy lips I shall gain my end."

"What is, then, a bond? And how has this bond come?
What cause has it? And how can one be free?"

"What is not-Self and what is the Higher Self?
And how can one discern between them?"

THE MASTER ANSWERS

"Happy art thou. Thou shalt attain thy end. Thy kin
is blest in thee. For thou seekest to become the Eternal
by freeing thyself from the bond of unwisdom."

"Sons and kin can pay a father's debts,
but none but a man's self can set him free."

"If a heavy burden presses on the head
others can remove it,
but none but a man's self can quench his hunger and thirst."

"Health is gained by the sick who follow the path of
healing: health does not come through the acts of others."

"The knowledge of the real by the eye of clear insight
is to be gained by one's own sight and not by the teacher's."

"The moon's form must be seen by one's own eyes;
it can never be known through the eyes of another."

"None but a man's self is able to untie the knots of
unwisdom, desire, and former acts, even in a myriad of ages."

"Freedom is won by a perception of the Self's oneness
with the Eternal, and not by the doctrines of Union
or of Numbers, nor by rites and sciences."

"The form and beauty of the lyre and excellent skill
upon its strings may give delight to the people,
but will never found an empire."

"An eloquent voice, a stream of words,
skill in explaining the teaching,
and the learning of the learned;
these bring enjoyment but not freedom."

"When the Great Reality is not known the study
of the scriptures is fruitless; when the Great Reality is known
the study of the scriptures is also fruitless."

"A net of words is a great forest
where the fancy wanders; therefore the reality of the Self
is to be strenuously learned from the knower of that reality."

"How can the hymns (Vedas) and the scriptures
profit him who is bitten by the serpent of unwisdom?
How can charms or medicine help him without the medicine
of the knowledge of the Eternal?"

"Sickness is not cured by saying 'Medicine,'
but by drinking it.
So a man is not set free by the name of the Eternal
without discerning the Eternal."

"Without piercing through the visible,
without knowing the reality of the Self, how can men gain
Freedom by mere outward words that end with utterances?"

"Can a man be king by saying, 'I am king,'
without destroying his enemies,
without gaining power over the whole land?"

"Through information, digging,
and casting aside the stones, a treasure may be found,
but not by calling it to come forth."

"So by steady effort is gained the knowledge
of those who know the Eternal,
the lonely, stainless reality above all illusion;
but not by desultory study."

"Hence with all earnest effort
to be free from the bondage of the world,
the wise must strive themselves,
as they would to be free from sickness."

"And this question put by thee today must be solved by
those who seek Freedom; this question that breathes the spirit
of the teaching, that is like a clue with hidden meaning."

"Hear, then, earnestly, thou wise one,
the answer given by me; for by understanding it
thou shalt be free from the bondage of the world."

SELF, POTENCIES, VESTURES

The first cause of Freedom is declared to be
an utter turning back from lust after unenduring things.
Thereafter Restfulness, Control, Endurance;
a perfect Renouncing of all acts that cling and stain.

Thereafter, the divine Word, a turning of the mind to it,
a constant thinking on it by the pure one,
long and uninterrupted.

Then ridding himself altogether of doubt,
and reaching wisdom,
even here he enjoys the bliss of Nirvana.

Then the discerning between Self and not-Self
that you must now awaken to, that I now declare,
hearing it, lay hold on it within yourself.

THE VESTURES

(Verses 72 – 107)

Formed of the substances they call marrow, bone, fat, flesh, blood, skin and over-skin; fitted with greater and lesser limbs, feet, breast, trunk, arms, back, head; this is called the physical vesture by the wise – the vesture whose authority, as "I" and "my" is declared to be a delusion.

Then these are the refined elements:
the ethereal, the upper air, the flaming, water, and earth.

These when mingled one with another become the physical elements, that are the causes of the physical vesture. The materials of them become the five sensuous things that are for the delight of the enjoyer – sounds and other things of sense.

They who, fooled in these sensuous things, are bound by the wide noose of lust, hard to break asunder – they come and go, downwards and upwards on high, led by the swift messenger, their works.

Through the five sensuous things five creatures find dissolution to the five elements, each one bound by his own character: the deer, the elephant, the moth, the fish, the bee; what then of man, who is snared by all the five?

Sensuous things are keener to injure than the black snake's venom; poison slays only him who eats it, but these things slay him who only beholds them with his eyes.

He who is free from the great snare,
so hard to be rid of, of longing after sensuous things,
he indeed builds for Freedom, and not another,
even though knowing the six philosophies.

Those who, only for a little while rid of lust,
long to be free,
and struggle to reach the shore of the world-ocean –
the toothed beast of longing lust makes them sink half way,
seizing them by the throat, and swiftly carrying them away.

By whom this toothed beast called sensuous things is
slain by the sharp sword of true turning away from lust,
he reaches the world-sea's shore without hindrance. He who,
soul-destroyed, treads the rough path of sensuous things,
death is his reward, like him who goes out on a luckless day.
But he who goes onward, through the word
of the good Teacher who is friendly to all beings,
and himself well-controlled, he gains the fruit and the reward,
and his reward is the Real.

If the love of Freedom is yours,
then put sensuous things far away from you, like poison.
But love, as the food of the gods, serenity, pity, pardon,
rectitude, peacefulness and self-control;
love them and honor them forever.

He who every moment
leaving undone what should be done
– the freeing of himself from the bonds
of beginningless unwisdom –
devotes himself to the fattening of his body,
that rightly exists for the good of the other powers,
such a one thereby destroys himself.

He who seeks to behold the Self,
although living to fatten his body, is going to cross the river,
holding to a toothed beast, while thinking it a tree.

For this delusion for the body and its delights
is a great death for him who longs for Freedom;
the delusion by the overcoming of which
he grows worthy of the dwelling-place of the free.

Destroy this great death,
this infatuation for the body, wives and sons; conquering it,
the pure ones reach the Pervader's supreme abode.

This faulty form, built up of skin and flesh,
of blood and sinews, fat and marrow and bones, gross and full
of impure elements; born of the fivefold physical elements
through deeds done before, the physical place of enjoyment of
the Self; its mode is waking life, whereby there arises
experience of physical things.

Subservient to physical objects through the outer
powers, with its various joys – flower-chaplets, sandal, lovers
– the Life makes itself like this through the power of the Self;
therefore this form is pre-eminent in waking life.

But know that this physical body
wherein the whole circling life of the Spirit adheres,
is but as the dwelling of the lord of the dwelling.

Birth and age and death are the fate of the physical
and all the physical changes from childhood onward; of the
physical body only are caste and grade with their many homes,
and differences of worship and dishonor and great honor
belong to it alone.

The powers of knowing – hearing, touch, sight, smell,
taste – for apprehending sensuous things; the powers of doing
– voice, hands, feet, the powers that put forth and generate –
to effect deeds.

Then the inward activity: mind, soul, self-assertion,
imagination, with their proper powers; mind, ever intending
and doubting; soul, with its character of certainty as to things;
self-assertion, that falsely attributes the notion of "I";
imagination, with its power of gathering itself together,
and directing itself to its object.

These also are the life-breaths: the forward-life,
the downward-life, the distributing-life, the uniting-life;
their activities and forms are different,
as gold and water are different.

The subtle vesture they call the eightfold inner being
made up thus: voice and the other four, hearing and the other
four, ether and the other four, the forward life and the other
four, soul and the other inward activities, unwisdom,
desire and action.

Hear now about this subtle vesture or form vesture,
born of elements not fivefold; it is the place of gratification,
the enjoyer of the fruits of deeds, the beginningless disguise
of the Self, through lack of self-knowledge.

Dream-life is the mode of its expansion, where it shines
with reflected light, through the traces of its own impressions;
for in dream-life the knowing soul shines of itself through the
many and varied mind-pictures made during the waking-life.

Here the higher self shines of itself and rules, taking on
the condition of doer, with pure thought as its disguise,
an unaffected witness, nor is it stained by the actions,
there done, as it is not attached to them, therefore it is not
stained by actions, whatever they be, done by its disguise;
let this form-vesture be the minister doing the work of the
conscious self, the real man, just as the tools do the
carpenter's work; thus this self remains unattached.

Blindness or slowness or skill come from the goodness
or badness of the eye; deafness and dumbness are of the ear
and not of the Knower, the Self.

Up-breathing, down-breathing, yawning, sneezing,
the forward moving of breath, and the outward moving –
these are the doings of the life-breaths,
say those who know these things;
of the life-breaths, also, hunger and thirst are properties.

The inner activity dwells and shines in sight
and the other powers in the body,
through the false attribution of selfhood, as cause.

Self-assertion is to be known as the cause
of this false attribution of selfhood, as doer and enjoyer;
and through substance and the other two potencies,
it reaches expansion in the three modes.

When sensuous things have affinity with it, it is happy;
when the contrary, unhappy.
So happiness and unhappiness are properties of this,
and not of the Self which is perpetual bliss.

Sensuous things are dear for the sake of the self,
and not for their own sake;
and therefore the Self itself is dearest of all.

Hence the Self itself is perpetual bliss –
not for it are happiness and unhappiness; as in dreamless life,
where there are no sensuous things, the Self that is bliss –
is enjoyed, so in waking-life it is enjoyed through the word,
through intuition, teaching and deduction.

THE THREE POTENCIES

(Verses 108 – 135)

The power of the supreme Master,
that is called unmanifested, beginningless unwisdom
whose very self is the three potencies,
to be known through thought, by its workings –
this is glamour (Maya),
whereby all this moving world is made to grow.

Neither being nor non-being
nor of the self of both of these;
neither divided nor undivided nor of the self of both of these;
neither formed nor formless nor of the self of both of these –
very wonderful and ineffable is its form.

To be destroyed by the awakening to the pure,
secondless Eternal, as the serpent imagined in a rope,
when the rope is seen; its potencies are called substance,
force, and darkness; each of them known by their workings.
The self of doing belongs to force, whose power is extension,
whence the pre-existent activities issued; rage and all the
changes of the mind that cause sorrow are ever its results.

Desire, wrath, greed, vanity, malice, self-assertion,
jealousy, envy, are the terrible works of Force,
its activities in man; therefore this is the cause of bondage.

Then enveloping is the power of Darkness,
whereby a thing appears as something else;
this is the cause of the circling birth and rebirth of the spirit,
and the cause whereby extension is drawn forward.

Though a man be full of knowledge, learned, skillful,
very subtle-sighted, if Darkness has wrapped him round,
he sees not, though he be full of manifold instruction;
he calls good that which is raised by error,
and leans upon its properties, unlucky man that he is;
great and hard to end is the enveloping power of Darkness.

Wrong thinking, contradictory thinking,
fanciful thinking, confused thinking – these are its workings;
this power of extension never leaves hold
of one who has come into contact with it,
but perpetually sends him this way and that.

Unwisdom, sluggishness, inertness, sloth, infatuation,
folly, and things like these are of the potency of Darkness.
Under the yoke of these he knows nothing at all,
but remains as though asleep or like a post.

But the potency of substance is pure like water,
and even though mixed with the other two,
it builds for the true refuge;
for it is a reflected spark of the Self,
and lights up the inert like the sun.

Of the potency of Substance when mixed
the properties are self-respect, self-restraint, control,
faith and love and the longing to be free, a godlike power
and a turning back from the unreal.

Of the potency of substance altogether pure
the properties are grace, direct perception of the Self, and
perfect peace; exulting gladness, a resting on the Self supreme,
whereby he reaches the essence of real bliss.

The unmanifest is characterized by these three
potencies; it is the causal vesture of the Self; dreamless life is
the mode where it lives freely, all the activities of the powers,
and even of the knowing soul having sunk back into it.

Every form of outward perceiving has come to rest, the
knowing soul becomes latent in the Self from which it springs;
the name of this is dreamless life, wherein he says
"I know nothing at all of the noise of the moving world."

The body, powers, life-breaths, mind, self-assertion,
all changes, sensuous things, happiness, unhappiness,
the ether and all the elements,
the whole world up to the unmanifest – this is not Self.

Glamour and every work of glamour
from the world-soul to the body, know this as unreal,
as not the Self, built up of the mirage of the desert.

But I shall declare to you
the own being of the Self supreme, knowing which a man,
freed from his bonds, reaches the lonely purity.

There is a certain selfhood wherein the sense of "I"
forever rests; who witnesses the three modes of being,
who is other than the five veils;
who is the only knower in waking, dreaming, dreamlessness;
of all the activities of the knowing soul, whether good or bad –
this is the "I"; who of himself beholds all; whom none beholds;
who kindles to consciousness the knowing soul and all the
powers; whom none kindles to consciousness;

by whom all this is filled; whom no other fills;
who is the shining light within this all;
after whose shining all else shines; by whose nearness only
body and powers and mind and soul do their work each in his
own field, as though sent by the Self;
because of the own nature of this is eternal wakefulness,
self-assertion, the body and all the powers,
and happiness and unhappiness are beheld by it,
just as an earthen pot is beheld.
This inner Self, the ancient Spirit, is everlasting, partless,
immediately experienced happiness; ever of one nature,
pure waking knowledge,
sent forth by whom Voice and life-breaths move.

Here, verily, in the substantial Self, in the hidden place
of the soul, this steady shining begins to shine like the dawn;
then the shining shines forth as the noonday sun,
making all this world to shine by its inherent light;
knower of all the changing moods of mind and inward powers;
of all the acts done by the body, powers, life-breaths;
present in them as fire in iron, strives not nor changes at all.

This is not born nor dies nor grows,
nor does it fade or change forever;
even when this form has melted away,
it no more melts than the air in a jar.

Alike stranger to forming and deforming; of its own
being, pure wakefulness; both being and non-being is this,
besides it there is nothing else; this shines unchanging,
this Supreme Self gleams in waking, dream and dreamlessness
as "I", present as the witness of the knowing soul.

BONDAGE AND FREEDOM

(Verses 136 – 153)

Then, holding firmly the mind,
with the knowing soul at rest,
know your self within yourself face to face saying, "This am I."
The life-ocean, whose waves are birth and dying, is shoreless;
cross over it, fulfilling the end of being,
resting firm in the Eternal.

Thinking things not self are "I" –
this is bondage for a man; this, arising from unwisdom,
is the cause of falling into the weariness of birth and dying;
this is the cause that he feeds and anoints and guards this
form, thinking it the Self; the unreal, real; wrapping himself
in sensuous things as a silk-worm in his own threads.

The thought that what is not That is That
grows up in the fool through darkness;
because no discernment is there, it wells up,
as the thought that a rope is a snake;
thereupon a mighty multitude of fatuities fall on him who
accepts this error, for he who grasps the unreal is bound;
mark this, my companion.

By the power of wakefulness, partless, external,
secondless, the Self wells up with its endless lordship;
but this enveloping power wraps it round, born of Darkness,
as the dragon of eclipse envelops the rayed sun.

When the real Self with its stainless light recedes,
a man thinking "this body is I," calls it the Self;
then by lust and hate and all the potencies of bondage,
the great power of Force that they call extension
greatly afflicts him.

Torn by the gnawing of the toothed beast of great delusion; wandered from the Self,
accepting every changing mood of mind as himself, through this potency, in the shoreless ocean of birth and death,
full of the poison of sensuous things, sinking and rising,
he wanders, mean-minded, despicable-minded.

As a line of clouds, born of the sun's strong shining,
expands before the sun and hides it from sight,
so self-assertion, that has come into being through the Self,
expands before the Self and hides it from sight.
As when on an evil day the lord of day is swallowed up in thick, dark clouds, an ice-cold hurricane of wind, very terrible, afflicts the clouds in turns;
so when the Self is enveloped in impenetrable Darkness,
the keen power of extension drives with many afflictions
the man whose soul is deluded.

From those two powers a man's bondage comes;
deluded by them he errs, thinking the body is the Self.

Of the plant of birth and death, the seed is Darkness,
the sprout is the thought that the body is the Self,
the shoot is rage, the sap is deeds, the body is the stem, the life-breaths are the branches, the tops are the bodily powers, sensuous things are the flowers, sorrow is the fruit,
born of varied deeds and manifold;
and the Life is the bird that eats the fruit.

This bondage to what is not Self, rooted in unwisdom,
innate, made manifest without beginning or end,
gives life to the falling torrent of sorrow, of birth and death,
of sickness and old age.

Not by weapons nor arms, not by storm nor fire
nor by a myriad of deeds can this be cut off,
without the sword of discernment and knowledge,
very sharp and bright,
through the grace of the guiding power.

He who is single-minded, fixed on the word divine,
his steadfast fulfillment of duty
will make the knowing soul within him pure;
to him whose knowing soul is pure,
a knowing of the Self supreme shall come;
and through this knowledge of the Self supreme
he shall destroy this circle of birth and death
and its root together.

THE FREEING OF THE SELF

(Verses 148 – 154)

The Self, wrapped up in the five vestures
beginning with the vesture formed of food,
which are brought into being by its own power,
does not shine forth,
as the water in the pond, covered by a veil of green scum.

When the green scum is taken away,
immediately the water shines forth pure,
taking away thirst and heat,
straightway becoming a source of great joy to man.

When the five vestures have been stripped off,
the Self shines forth pure, the one essence of eternal bliss,
beheld within, supreme, self-luminous.

Discernment is to be made
between the Self and what is not Self
by the wise man seeking freedom from bondage;
through this he enters into joy,
knowing the Self which is being, consciousness, bliss.

As the reed from the tiger grass,
so separating from the congeries of things visible
the hidden Self within,
which is detached,
not involved in actions,
and dissolving all in the Self,
he who stands thus, has attained liberation.

26

THE VESTURE FORMED OF FOOD

(Verses 154 – 164)

The food-formed vesture is this body,
which comes into being through food, which lives by food,
which perishes without food.

It is formed of cuticle, skin, flesh, blood, bone, water;
this is not worthy to be the Self, eternally pure.

The Self was before birth or death, and now is;
how can it be born for the moment, fleeting,
unstable of nature, not unified, inert, beheld like a jar?
For the Self is the witness of all changes of form.

The body has hands and feet, not the Self;
though bodiless, yet because it is the Life,
because its power is indestructible,
it is controller, not controlled.

Since the Self is witness of the body,
its character, its acts, its states,
therefore the Self must be of another nature than the body.

A mass of wretchedness, clad in flesh,
full of impurity and evil, how can this body be the knower?
The Self is of another nature.

Of this compound of skin, flesh, fat, bone and water,
the man of deluded mind thinks, "This is I";
but he who is possessed of judgment knows that his true Self
is of another character, its nature transcendental.

The mind of the dullard thinks of the body, "This is I";
he who is more learned thinks,
"This is I," of the body and the separate self;
but he who has attained discernment and is wise
knows the true Self saying, "I am the Eternal."

Therefore, O thou of mind deluded,
put away the thought that this body is the Self,
this compound of skin, flesh, fat, bone and water;
discern the universal Self, the Eternal, changeless,
and enjoy supreme peace.

So long as the man of learning abandons not
the thought, founded on delusion, that "This is I,"
regarding the unenduring body and its powers,
so long there is no hope for his liberation,
though he possesses the knowledge of the Vedanta
and its sciences.

As thou hast no thought that "This is the Self,"
regarding the body's shadow, or the reflected form,
or the body seen in dream, or the shape imagined in the mind,
so let not this thought exist regarding the living body.

The thought that the body is the Self,
in the minds of men who discern not the real,
is the seed from which spring birth and death and sorrow;
therefore slay thou this thought with strong effort,
for when thou hast abandoned this thought
the longing for rebirth will cease.

THE VESTURE FORMED OF VITAL BREATH

(Verses 165 – 166)

The breath-formed vesture is formed by the life-breath
determined by the five powers of action;
through its power the food-formed vesture,
guided by the Self and sustained by food,
moves in all bodily acts.

Nor is this breath-formed vesture the Self,
since it is formed of the vital airs,
coming and going like the wind, moving within and without;
since it can in no wise discern between right and wrong,
between oneself and another, but is ever dependent.

THE VESTURE FORMED OF MIND

(Verses 167 – 183)

The mind-formed vesture is formed
of the powers of perception and the mind; it is the cause
of the distinction between the notions of "mine" and "I";
it is active in making a distinction of names and numbers;
as more potent, it pervades and dominates the former vesture.

The fire of the mind-formed vesture,
fed by the five powers of perception,
as though by five sacrificial priests,
with objects of sense like streams of melted butter,
blazing with the fuel of manifold sense-impressions,
sets the personality aflame.

For there is no unwisdom, except in the mind,
for the mind is unwisdom, the cause of the bondage to life;
when this is destroyed, all is destroyed;
when this dominates, the world dominates.

In dream, devoid of substance,
it emanates a world of experiencer and things experienced,
which is all mind; so in waking consciousness,
there is no difference, it is all the domination of the mind.

During the time of dreamlessness,
when the mind has become latent,
nothing at all of manifestation remains;
therefore man's circle of birth and death is built by mind,
and has no permanent reality.

By the wind a cloud is collected,
by the wind it is driven away again;
by mind bondage is built up, by mind is built also liberation.

Building up desire for the body and all objects,
it binds the man thereby as an ox by a cord;
afterwards leading him to turn from them like poison,
that same mind, verily, sets him free from bondage.

Therefore mind is the cause of man's bondage,
and in turn of his liberation;
when darkened by the powers of passion
it is the cause of bondage,
and when pure of passion and darkness
it is the cause of liberation.

Where discernment and dispassion are dominant,
gaining purity, the mind makes for liberation;
therefore let the wise man who seeks liberation
strengthen these two in himself as the first step.

Mind is the name of the mighty tiger
that hunts in the forest glades of sensuous things;
let not the wise go thither, who seek liberation.

Mind molds all sensuous things through
the earthly body and the subtle body of him who experiences;
mind ceaselessly shapes the differences of body, of color, of
condition, of race, as fruits caused by the acts of the potencies.

Mind, beclouding the detached, pure consciousness,
binding it with the cords of the body, the powers,
the life-breaths, as "I" and "my," ceaselessly strays
among the fruits of experience caused by its own activities.

Man's circle of birth and death
comes through the fault of attributing reality to the unreal,
but his false attribution is built up by mind;
this is the effective cause of birth and death and sorrow
for him who has the faults of passion and darkness
and is without discernment.

Therefore the wise who know the truth have declared
that mind is unwisdom, through which the whole world,
verily, is swept about, as cloud belts by the wind.

Therefore purification of the mind should be
undertaken with strong effort by him who seeks liberation;
when the mind has been purified,
liberation comes like fruit into his hand.

Through the sole power of liberation
uprooting desire for sensuous things,
and ridding himself of all bondage to works,
he who through faith in the Real stands firm in the teaching,
shakes off the very essence of passion from the understanding.

The mind-formed vesture cannot be the higher Self,
since it has beginning and end, waxing and waning;
by causing sensuous things, it is the very essence of pain;
that which is itself seen cannot be the Seer.

THE VESTURE FORMED OF INTELLIGENCE

(Verses 184 – 197)

The intelligence,
together with the powers of intelligence,
makes the intelligence-formed vesture,
whose distinguishing character is actor-ship;
it is the cause of man's circle of birth and death.

The power which is a reflected beam
of pure Consciousness, called the understanding,
is a mode of abstract nature;
it possesses wisdom and creative power;
it thereby focuses the idea of "I" in the body and its powers.

This "I," beginningless in time, is the separate self,
it is the initiator of all undertakings;
this, impelled by previous imprints,
works all works both holy and unholy, and forms their fruits.

Passing through varying births it gains experience,
now descending, now ascending;
of this intelligence-formed vesture,
waking, dream and dreamlessness
are the fields where it experiences pleasure and pain.

By constantly attributing to itself the body, state,
condition, duties and works, thinking, "These are mine,"
this intelligence-formed vesture,
brightly shining because it stands closest to the higher Self,
becomes the vesture of the Self,
and, thinking itself to be the Self,
wanders in the circle of birth and death.

This, formed of intelligence,
is the light that shines in the vital breaths, in the heart;
the Self who stands forever
wears this vesture as actor and experiencer.

The Self, assuming the limitation of the intelligence,
self-deluded by the error of the intelligence,
though it is the universal Self,
yet views itself as separate from the Self;
as the potter views the jars as separate from the clay.

Through the force of its union with the vesture,
the higher Self takes on the character of the vesture
and assumes its nature, as fire, which is without form,
takes on the varying forms of the iron,
even though the Self is for ever by nature
uniform and supreme.

THE DISCIPLE SPEAKS

Whether by delusion or otherwise,
the higher Self appears as the separate self;
but, since the vesture is beginningless,
there is no conceivable end of the beginningless.

Therefore existence as the separate self must be eternal,
nor can the circle of birth and death have an end;
how then can there be liberation?
Master, tell me this.

THE MASTER ANSWERS

Well hast thou asked, O wise one!
Therefore rightly hear!
A false imagination created by error is not conclusive proof.

Only through delusion
can there be an association with objects,
of that which is without attachment, without action, without
form; it is like the association of blueness with the sky.

The appearance as the separate self,
of the Self, the Seer, who is without qualities, without form;
essential wisdom and bliss,
arises through the delusion of the understanding; it is not real;
when the delusion passes, it exists no longer,
having no substantial reality.

Its existence,
which is brought into being through false perception,
because of delusion, lasts only so long as the error lasts;
as the serpent in the rope endures
only as long as the delusion;
when the delusion ceases,
there is no serpent.

THE WITNESS

THE MANIFEST AND THE HIDDEN SELF

(Verses 198 – 209)

Beginningless is unwisdom, and all its works are too;
but when wisdom is arisen, what belongs to unwisdom,
although beginningless – like a dream on waking – perishes,
root and all; though beginningless, it is not endless;
it is as something that was not before, and now is,
this is manifest.

It is thus seen that, though without a beginning,
unwisdom comes to an end,
just as something which before was not, comes into being.
Built up in the Self by its being bound by the disguise
of the intellect – is this existence as the separate life –
for there is no other than the Self,
distinguished by its own nature,
but the binding of the Self by the intellect is false,
coming from unknowledge.

This binding is untied by perfect knowledge,
not otherwise;
the discerning of the oneness of the Eternal and the Self
is held by the scripture to be perfect knowledge.

And this is accomplished
by perfectly discerning between Self and not-self;
thereafter discernment is to be gained
between individual and universal Self.

Water may be endlessly muddy,
but when the mud is gone, the water is clear.
As it shines, so shines the Self also,
when faults are gone away, it shines forth clear.

And when unreality ceases to exist
in the individual self,
it is clear that it returns towards the universal;
hence there is to be a rejection of the self-assertion
and other characteristics of the individual self.

Hence this higher Self
is not what is called the intellectual veil,
because that is changeful, helpless of itself,
circumscribed, objective, liable to err;
the non-eternal cannot be regarded as eternal.

The bliss-formed veil
is a form containing the reflection of bliss –
although it is tainted with darkness;
it has the quality of pleasure,
the attainment of well wished-for aims;
it shines forth in the enjoyment of good works
by a righteous man, of its own nature bliss-formed;
gaining an excellent form, he enjoys bliss without effort.

The principal sphere of the bliss-formed veil
is in dreamless sleep;
in dreaming and waking it is in part manifest
when blissful objects are beheld.

Nor is this bliss-formed veil the higher Self,
for it wears a disguise, it is a form of objective nature;
it is an effect caused by good acts,
accumulated in this changeful form.

When the five veils are taken away,
according to inference and scripture,
what remains after they are taken away is the Witness,
in a form born of awakening.

This is the Self, self-shining,
distinguished from the five veils;
this is the Witness in the three modes of perceiving,
without change, without stain.
The wise should know it as Being and Bliss, as his own Self.

THE PUPIL SAID:

(Verses 210 – 240)

When the five veils are thus set aside through their
unreality, beyond the non-being of all I see nothing, Master;
what then is to be known as anything
by him who knows Self and not-self?

THE MASTER SAID:

Truth has been spoken by thee, wise one;
thou art skilled in judgment.
Self-assertion and all these changes;
in the Self they have no being.
That whereby all is enjoyed, but which is itself not enjoyed,
know that to be the Self, the Knower,
through thy very subtle intellect.

Whatever is enjoyed by anyone,
of that he is the witness;
but of that which is not enjoyed by anyone,
it cannot be said that anyone is the witness.

That is to be self-witness,
where anything is enjoyed by itself;
therefore the universal Self is witness of itself;
no other lesser thing is witness of it.

In waking, dreaming, dreamlessness,
that Self is clearly manifested,
appearing through its universal form always as "I,"
as the "I" within, uniformly. This is "I" beholding intellect
and the rest that partake of varied forms and changes.
It is manifest through eternal blissful self-consciousness;
know that as the Self here in the heart.

Looking at the reflection of the sun
reflected in the water of a jar,
he who is deluded thinks it is the sun,
thus the reflected consciousness appearing under a disguise
is thought by him who is hopelessly deluded to be "I."

Rejecting the jar and water and the sun reflected there
all together, the real sun is beheld.
So the unchanging One which is reflected in the three modes,
self-shining, is perceived by the wise.

Putting away in thought body and intellect
as alike reflections of consciousness,
discerning the seer, hid in the secret place,
the Self, the partless awakening, the universal shining,
distinguished alike from what exists and what does not exist;
the eternal lord, all-present, very subtle,
devoid of within and without, nothing but Self;
discerning this perfectly, in its own form,
a man is sinless, passionless, deathless.

Sorrowless, altogether bliss, full of wisdom,
fearing nothing at all from anything;
there is no other path of freedom
from the bondage of the world
but knowledge of the reality of his Self,
for him who would be free.

Knowledge that the Eternal is not divided from him
is the cause of freedom from the world, whereby the Eternal,
the secondless bliss, is gained by the awakened.

Therefore one should perfectly know
that the Eternal and the Self are not divided;
for the wise who has become the Eternal
does not return again to birth and death.

The real, wisdom, the endless, the Eternal, pure,
supreme, self-perfect, the one essence of eternal bliss,
universal, undivided, unbroken – this he gains.

This is the real, supreme, secondless,
for besides the Self no other is;
there is nothing else at all
in the condition of perfect awakening
to the reality of the supreme being.

This all, that is perceived as the vari-form world,
from unknowledge, this all is the Eternal,
when the mind's confusion is cast away.

The pot made of clay is not separate from the clay,
for all through it, it is in its own nature clay;
the form of the pot is not separate; whence then the pot?
It is mere name, built up of illusion.

By no one can the form of the pot be seen,
separate from the clay; hence the pot is built of delusion,
but the real thing is the clay, like the supreme Being.

All this is always an effect of the real Eternal;
it is that alone, nor is there anything else but that.
He who says there is, is not free from delusion,
like one who talks in his sleep.

The Eternal verily is this all;
thus says the excellent scripture of the Atharva.
In accordance with it, all this is the Eternal only, nor is there
any separate existence of the attribute apart from the source.

If this moving world were the real,
then had the Self no freedom from limitation,
divine authority no worth, the Master Self no truth;
these three things the great souled cannot allow.

The Master who knows the reality of things declared:
I verily am not contained in these things,
nor do these creatures stand in me.
If the world be real,
then it should be apprehended in dreamless sleep; it is not
apprehended there, therefore it is unreal, dreamlike, false.
Therefore the world is not separate from the higher Self;
what is perceived as separate is false –
the natural potencies and the like;
what real existence is there in the attribute?
Its support shines forth as with attributes illusively.

Whatever is delusively perceived by one deluded,
is the Eternal; the silver shining is only the pearl shell.
The Eternal is perpetually conceived as formed;
but what is attributed to the Eternal is a name only.

Therefore the supreme Eternal is Being, secondless,
of the form of pure knowledge, stainless, peaceful,
free from beginning or ending, changeless;
its own-nature is unbroken bliss.

Every difference made by world-glamour set aside,
eternal, lasting, partless, measureless, formless,
unmanifest, nameless, unfading,
a self-shining light that illuminates all that is.

Where the difference of knower, knowing, known
is gone, endless, sure; absolute, partless, pure consciousness;
the wise know this as the supreme reality.

That can neither be left nor taken,
is no object of mind or speech; immeasurable,
beginningless, endless, the perfect Eternal, the universal "I."

THAT THOU ART

(Verses 241 – 251)

The Eternal and the Self,
indicated by the two words "that" and "thou," when clearly
understood, according to the Scripture "THAT THOU ART,"
are one; their oneness is again ascertained.

This identity of theirs
is in their essential, not their verbal meanings,
for they are apparently of contradictory character;
like the firefly and the sun, the sovereign and the serf,
the well and the great waters, the atom and Mount Meru.

The contradiction between them is built up by their
disguises, but this disguise is no real thing at all; the disguise
of the Master Self is the world-glamour, the cause of the
Celestial and other worlds; the disguise of the individual life is
the group of five veils – hear this now: These are the two
disguises, of the Supreme and the individual life; when they
are set aside together, there is no longer the Supreme nor the
individual life.

The king has his kingdom, the warrior his weapons; when
these are put away there is neither warrior nor king.

According to the scripture saying,
"this is the instruction, the Self is not that, not that,"
the twofoldness that was built up
sinks away of itself in the Eternal;
let the truth of this scripture be grasped through awakening;
the putting away of the two disguises
must verily be accomplished.

It is not this, it is not this:
because this is built up, it is not the real –
like the serpent seen in the rope, or like a dream;
thus putting away every visible thing by wise meditation,
the oneness of the two – the Self and the Eternal –
is then to be known.

Therefore the two are to be well observed
in their essential unity. Neither their contradictory character
nor their non-contradictory character is all;
but the real and essential Being is to be reached,
in order to gain the essence
in which they are one and undivided.

When one says: "This man is Devadatta,"
the oneness is here stated by rejecting contradictory qualities.
With the great word "THAT THOU ART," it is the same;
what is contradictory between the two is set aside.

As being essentially pure consciousness,
the oneness between the Real and the Self
is known by the awakened;
and by hundreds of great texts
the oneness, the absence of separateness,
between the Eternal and the Self is declared.

That is not the physical; it is the perfect,
after the unreal is put aside;
like the ether, not to be handled by thought.

40

Hence this matter that is perceived is illusive,
therefore set it aside;
but what is grasped by its own selfhood
– "that I am the Eternal" –
know that with intelligence purified;
know the Self as partless awakening.

Every Pot and vessel has always clay as its cause,
and its material is clay;
just like this, this world is engendered by the Real,
and has the Real as its Self, the Real is its material altogether.
That Real than which there is none higher, THAT THOU ART,
the restful, the stainless, secondless Eternal, the supreme.

THE MANIFEST AND THE HIDDEN SELF

(Verses 252 – 268)

As dream-built lands and times,
objects and knowers of them, are all unreal,
just so here in waking is this world;
its cause is ignorance of the Self; in as much as all this world,
body and organs, vital breath and personality are all unreal,
in so much THOU ART THAT,
the restful, the stainless, secondless Eternal, the supreme.

Far away from birth and conduct, family and tribe,
quite free from name and form and quality and fault;
beyond space and time and objects –
this is the Eternal, THAT THOU ART; become it in the Self.

The supreme, that no word can reach,
but that is reached by the eye of awakening, pure of stain,
the pure reality of consciousness and mind together –
this is the Eternal, THAT THOU ART; become it in the Self.

Untouched by the six infirmities,
reached in the heart of those that seek for union,
reached not by the organs,
whose being neither intellect nor reason knows –
this is the Eternal, THAT THOU ART; become it in the Self.

Built of error is the world; in That it rests;
That rests in itself,
different from the existent and the non-existent;
partless, nor bound by causality,
is the Eternal, THAT THOU ART; become it in the Self.

Birth and growth, decline and loss, sickness and death
it is free from, and unfading;
the cause of emanation, preservation, destruction,
is the Eternal, THAT THOU ART; become it in the Self.

Where all difference is cast aside,
all distinction is cast away, a waveless ocean, motionless;
ever free, with undivided form –
this is the Eternal, THAT THOU ART; become it in the Self.

Being one, though cause of many, the cause of others,
with no cause itself;
where cause and caused are merged in one, self-being,
the Eternal, THAT THOU ART; become it in the Self.

Free from doubt and change, great, unchanging;
where changing and unchanging are merged in one Supreme;
eternal, unfading joy, unstained –
this is the Eternal, THAT THOU ART; become it in the Self.

This shines forth manifold through error, through
being the Self under name and form and quality and change;
like gold itself unchanging ever –
this is the Eternal, THAT THOU ART; become it in the Self.

This shines out unchanging, higher than the highest,
the hidden one essence, whose character is selfhood, reality,
consciousness, joy, endless unfading –
this is the Eternal, THAT THOU ART; become it in the Self.

Let a man make it his own in the Self –
like a word that is spoken, by reasoning from the known,
by thought; this is as devoid of doubt as water in the hand,
so certain will its reality become.

Recognizing this perfectly illumined one,
whose reality is altogether pure,
as one recognizes the leader of men in the assembled army,
and resting on that always, standing firm on one's own Self,
sink all this world that is born, into the Eternal.

In the soul, in the hidden place,
marked neither as what is nor what is not,
is the Eternal, true, supreme, secondless.
He who through the Self dwells here in the secret place,
for him there is no coming forth again to the world of form.

When the thing is well known even,
this beginningless mode of thought,
"I am the doer and the enjoyer," is very powerful;
this mode of mind lasting strongly,
is the cause of birth and rebirth.
A looking backward toward the Self, a dwelling on it,
is to be effortfully gained;
freedom here on earth, say the saints,
is the thinning away of that mode of thought.

That thought of 'I' and 'mine'
in the flesh, the eye and the rest, that are not the Self –
this transference from the real to the unreal
is to be cast away by the wise man
by steadfastness in his own Self.

FINDING THE REAL SELF

BONDAGE THROUGH IMAGINATION

(Verses 269 – 276)

Recognizing as thine own the hidden Self,
the witness of the soul and its activities,
perceiving truly "That am I,"
destroy the thought of Self in all not Self.

Give up following after the world,
give up following after the body,
give up following after the ritual law;
make an end of transferring selfhood to these.

Through a man's imagination being full of the world,
through his imagination being full of the ritual law,
through his imagination being full of the body –
wisdom, truly, is not born in him.

For him who seeks freedom
from the grasping hand of birth and death,
an iron fetter binding his feet, say they who know it,
is this potent triad of imaginings;
he who has got free from this enters into freedom.

The scent of sandalwood that drives all evil odors away
comes forth through stirring it with water and the like;
all other odors are driven altogether away.

The image of the supreme Self,
stained by the dust of imaginings, dwelling inwardly, endless,
evil, comes forth pure, by the stirring power of enlightenment,
as the scent of the sandalwood comes forth clear.

In the net of imaginings of things not Self,
the image of the Self is held back;
by resting on the eternal Self, their destruction comes,
and the Self shines clear.

As the mind rests more and more on the Self behind it,
it is more and more freed from outward imaginings;
when imaginings are put away,
and no residue left,
he enters and becomes the Self,
pure of all bonds.

SELFHOOD TRANSFERRED TO THINGS NOT SELF

(Verses 277 – 298)

By resting ever in the Self,
the restless mind of him who seeks union is stilled,
and all imaginings fade away;
therefore make an end of transferring Selfhood
to things not Self.

Darkness is put away through force
and substantial being; force, through substantial being;
in the pure, substantial being is not put away; therefore,
relying on substantial being,
make an end of transferring selfhood to things not Self.

The body of desire is nourished
by all new works begun; steadily thinking on this,
and effortfully holding desire firm,
make an end of transferring selfhood to things not Self.

Thinking:
"I am not this separate life but the supreme Eternal,"
beginning by rejecting all but this,
make an end of transferring selfhood to things not Self;
it comes from the swift impetus of imaginings.

Understanding the all-selfhood of the Self,
by learning, seeking union, entering the Self,
make an end of transferring selfhood to things not Self;
it comes from the Self's reflected light in other things.

Neither in taking nor giving does the sage act at all;
therefore by ever resting on the One,
make an end of transferring selfhood to things not Self.

Through sentences like "That thou art"
awaking to the oneness of the Eternal and the Self,
to confirm the Self in the Eternal,
make an end of transferring selfhood to things not Self.

While there yet lingers a residue undissolved
of the thought that this body is the Self,
carefully seeking union with the Self,
make an end of transferring selfhood to things not Self.

As long as the thought of separate life
and the world shines, dreamlike even,
so long incessantly, O wise one,
make an end of transferring selfhood to things not Self.

The body of desire,
born of father and mother of impure elements,
made up of fleshly things impure,
is to be abandoned as one abandons an impure man afar;
gain thy end by becoming the Eternal.

THE REAL IN THINGS UNREAL

As the space in a jar in universal space,
so the Self is to be merged without division
in the Self supreme; rest thou ever thus, O sage.

Through the separate self gaining the Self,
self-shining as a resting-place,
let all outward things from a world-system to a lump of clay
be abandoned, like a vessel of impure water.

Raising the thought of "I" from the body
to the Self that is Consciousness, Being, Bliss,
and lodging it there, leave form, and become pure for ever.

Knowing that "I am that Eternal"
wherein this world is reflected, like a city in a mirror,
thou shalt perfectly gain thy end.

What is of real nature, self-formed,
original consciousness, secondless bliss, formless, actless —
entering that, let a man put off this false body of desires,
worn by the Self as a player puts on a costume.

For the Self, all that is seen is but a mirage;
it lasts but for a moment, we see, and know it is not "I";
how could "I know all" be said of the personal self
that changes every moment?

The real "I"
is witness of the personal self and its powers;
as its being is perceived always, even in dreamless sleep.
The scripture says the Self is unborn, everlasting;
this is the hidden Self, distinguished neither as what exists
nor what has no existence.

The beholder of every change in things that change,
can be the unchanging alone;
in the mind's desires, in dreams, in dreamless sleep
the insubstantial nature of things that change
is clearly perceived again and again.

Therefore put away the false selfhood of this fleshly
body, for the false selfhood of the body is built up by thought;
knowing the Self as thine own, unhurt by the three times,
undivided illumination, enter into peace.

Put away the false selfhood of family and race
and name, of form and rank, for these dwell in this body;
put away the actorhood and other powers of the body of form;
become the Self whose self is partless joy.

Other bonds of man are seen, causes of birth and death,
but the root and first form of them is selfishness.

THE POWER OF MIND-IMAGES

(Verses 299 – 378)

As long as the Self is in bondage
to the false personal self of evil,
so long is there not even a possibility of freedom,
for these two are contraries.

But when free from the grasp of selfish personality,
he reaches his real nature;
Bliss and Being shine forth by their own light,
like the full moon, free from blackness.

But he who in the body thinks "this am I,"
a delusion built up by the mind through darkness;
when this delusion is destroyed for him without remainder,
there arises for him the realization of the Self as the Eternal,
free from all bondage.

The treasure of the bliss of the Eternal
is guarded by the terrible serpent of personality,
very powerful, enveloping the Self, with three fierce heads –
the three nature-powers; cutting off these three heads with the
great sword of discernment, guided by the divine teachings,
and destroying the serpent,
the wise man may enter into that joy-bringing treasure.

So long as there is even a trace of the taint of poison
in the body, how can there be freedom from sickness?
In just the same way, there is no freedom for him
who seeks union, while selfishness endures.

When the false self ceases utterly,
and the motions of the mind caused by it come to an end,
then, by discerning the hidden Self,
the real truth that "I am that" is found.

Give up at once the thought of "I"
in the action of the selfish personality, in the changeful self,
which is but a reflection of the real Self,
destroying it rest in the Self; from falsely attributing reality
to which are incurred birth and death and old age,
fruitful in sorrow, the pilgrimage of the soul;
but reality belongs to the hidden Self,
whose form is consciousness, whose body is bliss;
whose nature is ever one, the conscious Self, the Master,
whose form is Bliss, whose glory is unspeakable;
there is no cause of the soul's pilgrimage but
the attribution of the reality of this to the selfish personality.

Therefore this selfish personality, the enemy of the Self,
like a thorn in the throat of the eater,
being cut away by the great sword of knowledge,
thou shalt enjoy the bliss of the Self's sovereignty,
according to thy desire.

Therefore bringing to an end
the activity of the selfish personality,
all passion being laid aside when the supreme object is gained,
rest silent, enjoying the bliss of the Self, in the Eternal,
through the perfect Self, from all doubt free.

Mighty selfishness, even though cut down root and all,
if brought to life again even for a moment, in thought,
causes a hundred dissipations of energy,
as a cloud shaken by the wind in the rainy seasons,
pours forth its floods.

After seizing the enemy, selfishness,
no respite at all is to be given to it,
by thoughts of sensual objects.
Just this is the cause of its coming to life again,
as water is of the lime tree that had withered away.

The desirer is constituted by the bodily self;
how can the cause of desire be different?
Hence the motion of enticement to sensual objects
is the cause of world-bondage,
through attachment to what is other than the Self.

From increase of action,
it is seen that the seed of bondage is energized;
when action is destroyed, the seed is destroyed.
Hence let him check sensual action.

From the growth of mind-images comes the action;
from action the mind-image grows;
hence the man's pilgrimage ceases not.

To cut the bonds of the world's pilgrimage,
both must be burned away by the ascetic.
And the growth of mind-images comes from these two –
imagining and external action.

Growing from these two,
it brings forth the pilgrimage of the soul.
The way of destroying these three
in every mode of consciousness,
should be constantly sought.

By looking on all as the Eternal,
everywhere, in every way,
and by strengthening the mind-image of real being,
this triad comes to melt away.

In the destruction of actions
will arise the destruction of imaginings,
and from this the dispersal of mind-images.
The thorough dispersal of mind-images is freedom;
this is called freedom even in life.

When the mind-image of the real grows up,
in the dispersal of the mind's alarms,
and the mind-image of the selfish personality melts away,
as even thick darkness is quickly melted away
before the light of the sun.

The action of the greatest darkness,
the snare of unreality,
is no longer seen when the lord of day is arisen;
so in the shining of the essence of secondless bliss,
no bond exists nor scent of sorrow.

Transcending every visible object of sense,
fixing the mind on pure being, the totality of bliss,
with right intentness within and without,
pass the time while the bonds of action last.

Wavering in reliance on the Eternal must never be
allowed; wavering is death – thus said the son of the Evolver.

There is no other danger for him who knows
but this wavering as to the Self's real nature.
Thence arises delusion, and thence selfish personality;
thence comes bondage, and therefrom sorrow.

Through beholding sensual objects,
forgetfulness bewilders a wise man even,
as a woman her favorite lover.

As sedge pushed back
does not remain even for a moment,
just in the same way does the world-glamour
close over a wise man, who looks away from the Real.

If the imagination falling even a little from its aim,
towards outward objects,
it falls on and on, through unsteadiness,
like a player's ball fallen on a row of steps.

If the thought enters into sensual objects,
it becomes intent on their qualities;
from this intentness immediately arises desire,
and, from desire, every action of man.

Hence than this wavering there is no worse death,
for one who has gained discernment,
who has beheld the Eternal in spiritual concentration.
By right intentness he at once gains success;
be thou intent on the Self, with all carefulness.

Then comes loss of knowledge of one's real being,
and he who has lost it falls;
and destruction of him who thus falls is seen,
but not restoration.

Let him put away the willful motions of the mind,
the cause of every evil act;
he who has unity in life, has unity after his body is gone.
The scripture of sentences says that
he who beholds difference has fear.

Whenever even a wise man beholds difference
in the endless Eternal, though only as much as an atom,
what he beholds through wavering becomes a fear to him
through its difference.

All scripture, tradition and logic disregarding,
whoever makes the thought of self in visible things,
falls upon sorrow after sorrow;
thus disregarding, he is like a thief in darkness.

He whose delight is attachment to the real,
freed, he gains the greatness of the Self, eternal;
but he who delights in attachment to the false, perishes;
this is seen in the case of the thief and him who is no thief.

The ascetic, who has put away the cause of bondage –
attachment to the unreal – stands in the vision of the Self,
saying, "this Self am I";
this resting in the Eternal, brings joy by experiencing it,
and takes away the supreme sorrow that we feel,
whose cause is unwisdom.

Attachment to the outward brings as its fruit
the perpetual increase of evil mind-images.
Knowing this and putting away outward things
by discernment,
let him place his attachment in the Self forever.

When the outward is checked,
there is restfulness from emotion;
when emotion is at rest, there is vision of the supreme Self.
When the Self is seen, the bondage of the world is destroyed;
the checking of the outward is the path of freedom.

Who, being learned,
discerning between real and unreal,
knowing the teaching of the scripture,
and beholding the supreme object with understanding,
would place his reliance on the unreal,
even though longing to be free –
like a child, compassing his own destruction.

There is no freedom for him
who is full of attachment to the body and its like;
for him who is free, there is no wish for the body and its like,
the dreamer is not awake, he who is awake dreams not;
for these things are the opposites of each other.

Knowing the Self as within and without,
in things stable and moving – discerning this through the Self,
through its comprehending all things –
putting off every disguise, and recognizing no division,
standing firm through the perfect Self – such a one is free.

Through the All-self
comes the cause of freedom from bondage;
than the being of the All-self there is no other cause;
and this arises when there is no grasping after the outer;
he gains the being of the All-self
by perpetually resting on the Self.

How should the cessation of grasping after the outer
not fail for him who, through the bodily self
remains with mind attached to enjoyment of outward objects,
and thus engages in action.
It can only be effortfully accomplished by those
who have renounced the sensual aims of all acts and rites,
who are perfected in resting on the eternal Self,
who know reality, who long for reality and bliss in the Self.

The scripture that speaks of
"him who is at peace, controlled,"
teaches the ecstasy of the ascetic,
whose work is the study of wisdom,
to the end of gaining the All-self.

The destruction of personality
which has risen up in power cannot be done at once,
even by the learned,
except those who are immovably fixed in the ecstasy
which no doubt can assail,
for the mind-images are of endless rebirth.

Blinding a man with the delusion
of belief in his personality, through the power that veils,
the power that propels casts him forth, through its potencies.

The victory over this compelling power
cannot be accomplished until the power that veils
has come to cessation with residue.
The power that veils is, through the force of its own nature,
destroyed, when the seer is discerned from what is seen,
as milk is distinguished from water.

Perfect discernment, born of clear awakening,
arises free from doubt, and pure of all bondage,
where there is no propelling power towards delusive objects,
once the division is made between
the real natures of the seer and what is seen;
he cuts the bonds of delusion that glamour makes,
and after that, there is no more pilgrimage for the free.

The flame of discernment of the oneness of the
higher and the lower, burns up the forest of unwisdom utterly.
What seed of the soul's pilgrimage can there be for him
who has gained being in which there is no duality?

And the cessation of the veiling power
arises from perfect knowledge;
the destruction of false knowledge is the cessation of the pain
engendered by the propelling power.

The triple error is understood
by knowing the real nature of the rope;
therefore the reality of things is to be known by the wise
to the end of freedom from bondage.

As iron from union with fire, so,
from union with the real, thought expands as material things;
hence the triple effect of this, seen in delusion, dream, desire,
is but a mirage.

Thence come all changing forms in nature
beginning with personality and ending with the body,
and all sensual objects;
these are unreal, because subject to change every moment;
but the Self never changes.

Consciousness, eternal, non-dual, partless, uniform,
witness of intellect and the rest,
different from existent and non-existent;
its real meaning is the idea of "I";
a union of being and bliss – this is the higher Self.

He who thus understands,
discerning the real from the unreal,
ascertaining reality by his own awakened vision,
knowing his own Self as partless awakening,
freed from these things reaches peace in the Self.

Then melts the heart's knot of unwisdom without
residue, when, through the ecstasy in which there is no doubt,
arises the vision of the non-dual Self.

Through the mind's fault
are built the thoughts of thou and I and this,
in the supreme Self which is non-dual,
and beyond which there is nothing;
but when ecstasy is reached,
all his doubts melt away through apprehension of the real.

Peaceful, controlled, possessing the supreme cessation,
perfect in endurance, entering into lasting ecstasy,
the ascetic makes the being of the All-self his own;
thereby burning up perfectly the doubts
that are born of the darkness of unwisdom,
he dwells in bliss in the form of the Eternal,
without deed or doubt.

They who rest on the Self that is consciousness,
who have put away the outward,
the imaginations of the ear and senses, and selfish personality,
they, verily, are free from the bonds and snares of the world,
but not they who only meditate on what others have seen.

The Self is divided by the division of its disguises;
when the disguises are removed, the Self is lonely and pure;
hence let the wise man work for the removal of the disguises
by resting in the ecstasy that is free from doubt.

Attracted by the Self
the man goes to the being of the Self by resting on it alone;
the grub, thinking on the bee, builds up the nature of the bee.

The grub, throwing off attachment to other forms, and
thinking intently on the bee, takes on the nature of the bee;
even thus he who seeks for union,
thinking intently on the reality of the supreme Self,
perfectly enters that Self, resting on it alone.

Very subtle, as it were, is the reality of the supreme Self,
nor can it be reached by gross vision;
by the exceedingly subtle state of ecstasy
it is to be known by those who are worthy,
whose minds are altogether pure.

As gold purified in the furnace,
rids itself of dross and reaches the quality of its own self,
so the mind ridding itself of the dross of substance,
force and darkness, through meditation, enters into reality.

When purified by
the power of uninterrupted intentness,
the mind is thus melted in the Eternal,
then ecstasy is purified of all doubt,
and of itself enjoys the essence of secondless bliss.

Through this ecstasy comes destruction
of the knot of accumulated mind-images,
destruction of all works; within and without,
for ever and altogether, the form of the Self becomes manifest,
without any effort at all.

Let him know that thinking
is a hundred times better than scripture;
that concentration, thinking the matter out,
is a hundred thousand times better than thinking;
that ecstasy free from doubt
is endlessly better than concentration.

Through unwavering ecstasy is clearly understood
the reality of the Eternal, fixed and sure.
This cannot be when other thoughts are confused with it,
by the motions of the mind.

Therefore with powers of sense controlled
enter in ecstasy into the hidden Self,
with mind at peace perpetually;
destroy the darkness made by beginningless unwisdom,
through the clear view of the oneness of the real.

The first door of union is the checking of the voice,
the cessation of grasping,
freedom from expectation and longing,
the character bent ever on the one end.

A centering of the mind on the one end,
is the cause of the cessation of sensuality;
control is the cause that puts an end to imaginings;
by peace, the mind-image of the personality is melted away;
from this arises unshaken enjoyment of the essence of bliss
in the Eternal for ever, for him who seeks union;
therefore the checking of the imagination
is ever to be practiced effortfully, O ascetic!

Hold the voice in the self, hold the self in the intellect,
hold the intellect in the witness of the intellect, and, merging
the witness in the perfect Self, enjoy supreme peace.

The seeker for union shares the nature of each disguise
– body, vital breath, sense, mind, intellect –
when his thoughts are fixed on that disguise.

When he ceases from this sharing,
the ascetic reaches perfect cessation and happiness,
and is plunged in the essence of Being and Bliss.

Renouncing inwardly, renouncing outwardly –
this is possible only for him who is free from passion;
and he who is free from passion
renounces all attachment within and without,
through the longing for freedom.

Outward attachment arises through sensual objects;
inward attachment, through personality.
Only he who, resting in the Eternal, is free from passion,
is able to give them up.
Freedom from passion and awakening
are the wings of the spirit.
O wise man, understand these two wings! For without them
you cannot rise to the crown of the tree of life.

Soul-vision belongs to him who is free from passion;
steady inspiration belongs to the soul-seer.
Freedom from bondage belongs to the reality of inspiration;
enjoyment of perpetual bliss belongs to the Self that is free.

I see no engenderer of happiness greater than
freedom from passion for him who is self-controlled;
if very pure inspiration of the Self be joined to it,
he enters into the sovereignty of self-dominion.
This is the door of young freedom everlasting.
There do thou ever fix thy consciousness on the real Self,
in all ways free from attachment to what is other than this,
for the sake of the better way.

Cut off all hope in sensual objects which are like poison,
the cause of death;
abandon all fancies of birth and family and social state;
put all ritual actions far away;
renounce the illusion of self-dwelling in the body,
center the consciousness on the Self.
Thou art the seer, thou art the stainless,
thou art in truth the supreme, secondless Eternal.

Firmly fixing the mind on the goal, the Eternal,
keeping the outward senses in their own place,
with form unmoved, heedless of the body's state,
entering into the oneness of Self and Eternal
by assimilating the Self and rising above all differences,
for ever drink the essence of the bliss of the Eternal in the Self.
What profit is there in other things that give no joy?

FREE EVEN IN LIFE

(Verses 379 – 438)

Ceasing to feed the imagination on things not Self,
full of darkness, causing sorrow,
bend the imagination on the Self, whose form is bliss,
the cause of freedom.

This is the self luminous, witness of all,
ever shining through the veil of the soul;
making the one aim this Self,
that is contrary of all things unreal,
realize it by identification with its partless nature.

Naming this from its undivided being,
its freedom from all other tendency,
let him know it clearly from being of the own nature of Self.

Firmly realizing self-hood in that,
abandoning self-hood in the selfish personality,
stand towards it as a disinterested onlooker
stands towards the fragment of a broken vase.

Entering the purified inner organ
into the witness whose nature is the Self,
who is pure awakening,
leading upward step by step to unmoving firmness,
let him then gain the vision of perfection.

Let him gain vision of the Self,
freed from all disguises built up by ignorance of the Self
– body, senses, vitality, emotion, personality –
the Self whose nature is partless and perfect
like universal ether.

The ether, freed from its hundred disguises
– water-pots, jars, corn-measures and the like –
is one and not divided,
thus also the pure supreme, freed from the personality, is one.

All disguises beginning with the Evolver
and ending with a log are mirage only;
therefore let him behold his own perfect Self,
standing in the Self's oneness.

Whatever by error is built up as different from that,
is in reality that only, not different from that.
When the error is destroyed,
the reality of the snake that was seen shines forth as the rope;
thus the own-nature of all is the Self.

The Evolver is the Self, the Pervader is the Self,
the Sky-lord is the Self, the Destroyer is the Self;
all this universe is the Self;
there is nothing but the Self.

Inward is the Self, outward is also the Self;
the Self is to the east, the Self is also to the west.
The Self is to the south, the Self is also to the north.
The Self is above, the Self is beneath.

Just as wave and foam, eddy and bubble are in
their own nature water; so, from the body to the personality,
all is consciousness, the pure essence of consciousness.

Being verily is all this world,
that is known of voice and mind,
there is nothing else than Being,
standing on nature's other shore.
Are cup and water-pot and jar anything but earth?
He who is deluded by the wine of glamour
speaks of "thou" and "I."

"When by repeated effort naught remains but this,"
the scripture says, declaring absence of duality,
to put an end to the false transference of reality.

Like the ether, free from darkness, free from wavering,
free from limits, free from motion, free from change;
having neither a within nor a without, having no other than it,
having no second, is the Self, the supreme Eternal;
what else is there to be known?

What more is there to be said?
The Eternal, the Life, the Self is seen here under many forms;
all in this world is the Eternal, the secondless Eternal;
the scripture says "I am the Eternal";
knowing this clearly, those whose minds are awakened,
who have abandoned the outward, becoming the Eternal,
dwell in the Self, which is extending consciousness and bliss.
This, verily, is sure.

Kill out desire that springs up through thought of self
in the body formed of darkness,
then violent passion in the formal body woven of the breath.
Knowing the Self whose fame is sung in the hymns,
who is eternal and formed of bliss,
stand in the being of the Eternal.

As long as the son of man enjoys this body of death,
he is impure;
from the enemies arises the weariness
that dwells in birth and death and sickness.
When he knows the pure Self of benign form, immovable,
then he is free from these;
thus says the scripture too.

When all delusive qualities attributed to the Self
are put away, the Self is the supreme eternal, perfect,
secondless, changeless.

When the activity of the imagination
comes to rest in the higher Self, the Eternal that wavers not,
then no more wavering is seen, and vain words only remain.

The belief in this world is built up of unreality.
In the one substance, changeless, formless, undifferentiated,
what separateness can exist?

In the one substance,
in which no difference of seer, seeing, seen exists;
which is changeless, formless, undifferentiated,
what separateness can exist?

In the one substance,
like the world-ocean full to overflowing, changeless, formless,
undifferentiated, whence can separateness come?

Where the cause of delusion melts away,
like darkness in light, in the secondless, supreme reality,
undifferentiated, what separateness can there be?

In the supreme reality, the very Self of oneness,
how could any word of difference dwell?
By whom is difference perceived
in purely blissful dreamlessness?

For this world no longer is,
whether past, present, or to come,
after awakening to the supreme reality,
in the real Self, the Eternal, from all wavering free.
The snake seen in the rope exists not,
nor even a drop of water in the desert mirage,
where the deer thirsts.

This duality is mere glamour,
for the supreme reality is not twofold; thus the scripture says,
and it is directly experienced in dreamlessness.

By the learned it has been perceived that the thing
attributed has no existence apart from the substance,
as in the case of the serpent and the rope.
The distinction comes to life through delusion.

This distinction has its root in imagining;
when imagining ceases it is no more.
Therefore bring imagination to rest in the higher Self
whose form is concealed.

In soul-vision the wise man perceives in his heart a
certain wide-extending awakening, whose form is pure bliss,
incomparable, the other shore, for ever free,
where is no desire, limitless as the ether, partless,
from wavering free, the perfect Eternal.

In soul-vision the wise man perceives in his heart
the reality free from growth and change,
whose being is beyond perception,
the essence of equalness, unequalled, immeasurable,
perfectly taught by the words of inspiration,
eternal, praised by us.

In soul-vision the wise man perceives in his heart
the unfading, undying reality,
which by its own being can know no setting,
like the shimmering water of the ocean, bearing no name,
where quality and change have sunk to rest,
eternal, peaceful, one.

Through intending the inner mind to it,
gain vision of the Self,
in its own form, the partless sovereignty.
Sever thy bonds that are stained with the stain of life,
and effortfully make thy manhood fruitful.

Standing in the Self, realize the Self in being,
the Self from every disguise set free,
Being, Consciousness, Bliss, the secondless;
thus shalt thou build no more for going forth.

The mighty soul no more regards this body,
cast aside like a corpse, seen to be but the shadow of the man,
come into being as his reflection,
through his entering into the result of his works.

Drawing near to the eternal, stainless awakening,
whose nature is bliss,
put very far away this disguise whose nature is inert and foul;
nor let it be remembered again at all,
for the remembrance of what has been cast forth
builds for disdain.

Burning this up with its root
in the flame of the real Self, the unwavering Eternal,
the wise man stands excellent as the Self,
through the Self which is eternal, pure, awakening bliss.

The body is strung on the thread of works already done,
and is impure as the blood of slaughtered kine;
whether it goes forward or stands,
the knower of reality regards it not again,
for his life is dissolved in the Eternal, the Self of bliss.

Knowing the partless bliss, the Self as his own self,
with what desire or from what cause
could the knower of reality cherish the body?

Of the perfect adept this is the fruit,
of the seeker for union, free even in life –
to taste without and within the essence of being and bliss
in the Self.

The fruit of cleanness is awakening,
the fruit of awakening is quiescence;
from realizing the bliss of the Self comes peace,
this fruit, verily, quiescence bears.

When the latter of these is absent,
the former is fruitless.
The supreme end is the incomparable enjoyment
of the Self's bliss.

The famed fruit of wisdom
is not to tremble before manifest misfortune.
The various works that were done in the season of delusion,
worthy of all blame – how could a man deign to do them
after discernment has been gained?

Let the fruit of wisdom be cessation from unreality,
a continuation therein is the fruit of unwisdom;
this is clearly seen.
If there be not this difference
between him who knows and him who knows not,
as in the presence of the mirage to the thirsty deer,
where is the manifest fruit of wisdom?

If the heart's knot of unwisdom
be destroyed without remainder,
how could sensual things cause continuance in unreality,
in him who has no desire?

When mind-images arise not
in the presence of sensual things, this is the limit of purity;
when the personal idea does not arise,
this is the limit of illumination.
When life-activity that has been dissolved
does not arise again, this is the limit of quiescence.

He whose thought is free from outward objects,
through standing ever in the nature of the Eternal,
who is as lightly concerned with the enjoyment
of sensual things followed by others as a sleeping child,
looking on this world as a land beheld in dream,
when consciousness comes back,
enjoying the fruit of endless holy deeds,
he is rich and worthy of honor in the world.

This sage,
standing firm in wisdom,
reaches Being and Bliss,
he is changeless,
free from all acts,
for his Self is dissolved in the Eternal.

65

Being that is plunged in the oneness of the Eternal
and the Self made pure,
that wavers not and is pure consciousness alone,
is called wisdom.

They say he stands firm in wisdom,
in whom this wisdom steadfastly dwells.
He in whom wisdom is firmly established,
who enjoys unbroken bliss,
by whom the manifested world is almost unheeded,
is called free even in life.

He who with thought dissolved is yet awake,
though free from the bondage of waking life,
whose illumination is free from impure mind-images,
he, verily, is called free even in life.

He who perceives that his soul's pilgrimage is ended,
who is free from disunion even while possessing division,
whose imagination is free from imaginings,
he, verily, is called free even in life.

He who even while this body exists,
regards it as a shadow,
who has no sense of personality or possessions –
these are the marks of him who is free in life.

Whose mind lingers not over the past,
nor goes out after the future,
when perfect equanimity is gained,
this is the mark of him who is free even in life.

In this world, whose very nature is full of differences,
where quality and defect are distinguished,
to regard all things everywhere as the same,
this is the mark of him who is free even in life.

Accepting wished and unwished objects
with equanimity in the Self,
and changing not in either event,
is the mark of him who is free even in life.

When the sage's imagination
is fixed on tasting the essence of the bliss of the Eternal, so
that he distinguishes not between what is within and without,
this is the mark of him who is free even in life.

Who is free from the thought of "I" and "my,"
in body and senses and their works,
who stands in equanimity,
bears the mark of one who is free even in life.

He who never identifies himself
with the body and senses,
nor separates himself in thought
from what is other than these,
bears the mark of one who is free even in life.

THE THREE KINDS OF WORKS

(Verses 439 – 468)

He who through wisdom discerns that there is
no division between the Eternal and the manifested world,
bears the mark of one who is free even in life.

Whose mind is even,
when honored by the good, or persecuted by the wicked,
bears the mark of one who is free even in life.

In whom all sensuous objects,
put forth by the supreme,
melt together like the rivers and streams
that enter the ocean's treasure house,
making no change at all,
since he and they are but the one being,
this sage self-conquered is set free.

For him who has understood the nature of the Eternal,
there is no return to birth and death as of old;
if such return there be,
then the nature of the Eternal was not known.

If they say he returns to birth and death
through the rush of old imaginings, this is not true;
for, from the knowledge of oneness,
imaginings lose all their power.

As the most lustful man
ceases from desire before his mother;
so, when the Eternal is known,
the wise cease from desire, through fullness of bliss.

The scripture says that,
even for him who profoundly meditates,
there is a going after outward things of sense,
on account of Works already entered on.

As long as there is the taste of pain and pleasure,
so long are there Works already entered on;
the fruits come from the acts that went before;
without these acts where would the fruits be?

From the knowledge that I am the Eternal,
the accumulated Works,
heaped up even through hundreds of myriads of ages,
melt away like the work of a dream, on awaking.

Whatever one does while dreaming,
however good or bad it seems,
what effect has it on him, on awaking
to send him either to hell or heaven?

On knowing the Self, unattached,
enthroned like the dome of heaven,
the man is no longer stained at all by Works to come.

As the ether enclosed in the jar
is not stained by the smell of the wine,
so the Self encompassed by its vestures,
is not stained by any quality of theirs.

Works that have been entered on,
before wisdom's sunrise, are not destroyed by wisdom,
until they have reached their fruition;
like an arrow aimed and sent forth at the mark.

The arrow discharged
by the thought that there was a tiger,
does not stop when it is seen to be a cow,
but pierces the mark through its exceeding swiftness.

Verily,
Works entered on are the most formidable to the wise,
they disappear only through being experienced.
But Works accumulated and Works to come both melt away
in the fire of perfect wisdom.

When they have beheld the oneness
of the Self and the Eternal,
and stand ever firm in the power of that knowledge,
for them those three kinds of Works exist no longer;
for them there is only the Eternal, free from every change.

When the saint rests in the Self,
through understanding that the Self is other than its vestures,
that the Self is the pure Eternal;
then the myth of the reality of Works entered on
no longer holds him,
just as the myth of union with things of dream
no longer holds him who has awakened.

For he who is awake
no longer keeps the sense of "I and mine and that,"
for his looking-glass body and the world that belongs to it;
but comes to himself merely through waking.

Neither a desire for pursuing mythical objects,
nor any grasping after even a world full of them,
is seen in him who has awakened.
But if the pursuit of mirages goes on,
then it is seen for certain
that the man has not wakened from sleep.

Thus dwelling in the supreme Eternal,
through the real Self, he stands and beholds naught else.
Like the memory of an object looked on in dream,
so is it, for the wise, with eating or the other acts of life.

The body is built up through Works;
the Works entered upon
make for the building up of various forms;
but the Self is not built up through works.

"Unborn, eternal, immemorial," says the Scripture,
whose words are not in vain; of him who rests in that Self,
what building up of Works entered on can there be?

Works entered upon flourish then,
when the Self is identified with the body;
but the identifying of the Self with the body brings no joy,
therefore let Works entered upon be renounced.

Even the building up of a body
through Works entered on is a mirage;
whence can come the reality of a mere reflected image?
Whence can come the birth of an unreality?

Whence can come the death
of what has not even been born?
Whence can come the entering on of what does not even exist
– if there be a melting away of the effects of unwisdom,
root and all, through the power of wisdom.

How does this body stand?
In the case of him who takes inert things to be real,
Works entered on are supported
by the sight of outward things – thus says the scripture;
yet it does not teach the reality of the body and the like,
to the wise.

One, verily, is the Eternal, without a second.
There is no difference at all.
Altogether perfect, without beginning or end,
measureless and without change.

The home of Being, the home of Consciousness,
the home of Bliss enduring, changeless;
one, verily, without a second, is the Eternal.
There is no difference at all.

Full of the pure essence of the unmanifested,
endless, at the crown of all;
one, verily, without a second, is the Eternal.
There is no difference at all.

That can neither be put away, nor sought after;
that can neither be taken nor approached –
one, verily, without a second, is the Eternal;
there is no difference at all.

Without qualities, without parts, subtle,
without wavering, without stain;
one, verily, without a second, is the Eternal;
there is no difference at all.

MASTER AND PUPIL

(Verses 469 – 518)

THE TEACHER SPEAKS:

That, whose nature no man can define;
where is no pasturage for mind or word;
one, verily, without second, is the Eternal;
there is no difference at all.

The fullness of Being,
self-perfect, pure, awakened, unlike aught here;
one, verily, without second, is the Eternal;
there is no difference at all!

They who have cast away passion,
who have cast away sensual delights,
peaceful, well-ruled, the sages, the mighty,
knowing reality in the supreme consummation,
have gained the highest joy in union with the Self.

Thou worthy one also,
seeking this higher reality of the Self,
whose whole nature is the fullness of bliss,
washing away the delusions thine own mind has built up,
be free, gaining thy end, perfectly awakened.

Through Soul-vision, through the self utterly unshaken,
behold the Self's reality, by the clear eye of awakening;
if the word of the scripture is perfectly perceived
without wavering, then doubt arises no more.

On gaining freedom
from the bonds bound by unwisdom as to the Self;
in the gaining of that Self
whose nature is truth, knowledge, bliss;
the holy books, reason, and the word of the guide
are one's evidences;
an evidence too is the realizing of the Self,
inwardly attained.

Freedom from bondage and joy,
health of thought and happiness,
are to be known by one's self;
the knowing of others is but inference.

As the teachers,
who have reached the further shore,
and the teachings tell,
let a man cross over through that enlightenment
which comes through the will of the higher Self.

Knowing the Self through one's own realization,
as one's own partless Self,
and being perfected,
let him stand firm in the unwavering Self.

This is the last and final word of the teaching:
The Eternal is the individual life and the whole world;
rest in the partless One is freedom,
in the Eternal, the secondless;
and this too the scriptures show.

Through the word of the Guide,
and the evidence of the teaching,
understanding the highest Being, through union with the Self,
he reached perfect peace, intent on the Self,
so that nothing could disturb him any more,
resting altogether in the Self.

Then after intending his mind for a while
on the supreme Eternal,
rising again from the highest bliss he spoke this word:

THE PUPIL SPEAKS:

Entangling thought has fallen away,
its activity has dissolved,
through mastery of the Self's oneness with the Eternal;
I know not this, nor anything that is not this; for what is it?
How great is it? Joy is its further shore.

This cannot be spoken by voice, nor thought by mind;
I taste the glory of the ocean of the Supreme Eternal,
filled full of the ambrosial bliss of the Self.
My mind, enjoying delight, like a watercourse,
that had dried up, when the multitude of waters come,
is full of happiness, even from the slightest portion
of the honey-sweet bliss of the Self.

Whither has this world of sorrow gone?
What has taken it away?
Whither has it dissolved?
Now I see that it no longer is – a mighty wonder!

What is there for me to reject? What to choose?
What else exists?
Where is there difference in the mighty ocean of the Eternal,
full of the nectar of partless bliss?

I see not, nor hear, nor know aught of this world;
for I bear the mark of the Self,
whose form is being and bliss.

Honor, honor to thee, my Guide, mighty-souled;
to thee, who art free from sensuous bondage,
who art most excellent, whose own nature is the essence
of the bliss of the secondless Everlasting,
whose words are ever a mighty, shoreless ocean of pity.

As one who was wearied with the heat,
bathing himself and refreshed,
in the enveloping light of the rayed moon,
thus I have in a moment gained the partless excellent bliss,
the imperishable word, the Self.

Rich am I, I have done what was to be done,
freed am I from the grasp of the sorrowing world.
My own being is everlasting bliss, I am filled full,
through the favor of the Self.

Unbound am I, formless am I, without distinction am I,
no longer able to be broken;
in perfect peace am I, and endless;
I am stainless, immemorial.

I am neither the doer nor enjoyer;
mine are neither change nor act.
I am in nature pure awakening.
I am the lonely One, august for ever.

I am apart from the personal self
that sees, hears, speaks, acts, and enjoys;
everlasting, innermost, without act;
the limitless, unbound, perfect Self awakened.

I am neither this nor that;
I am even he who illumines both, the supreme, the pure;
for me is neither inner nor outer,
for I am the perfect, secondless Eternal.

The unqualified, beginningless reality
is far from the thought of I and thou, of this and that;
I am the one essence of everlasting bliss,
the real, the secondless Eternal.

I am the Creator,
I am he who makes an end of hell,
he who makes an end of all things old;
I am the Spirit, I am the Lord;
I am partless awakening, the endless witness;
for me there is no longer any Lord,
no longer I nor mine.

For I, verily, consist in all beings,
enveloping them within and without,
through the Self that knows;
I myself am at once the enjoyer and all that is to be enjoyed –
whatever was seen before as separate –
through identity with it.

In me, the ocean of partless Bliss,
world-waves rise manifold, and fall again,
through the storm-winds of glamour's magic.

In me,
the material and other worlds are built up by glamour,
through swift vibrations;
just as in Time which has neither part nor division,
are built up the world-periods,
the years, the seasons, months, and days.

Nor does the Self,
on which the worlds are built,
become stained by them,
even through the deluded who are stained by many sins;
just as even a mighty flood of mirage waters
wets not the salt desert earth.

Like the ether, I spread throughout the world;
like the sun, I am marked by my shining;
like the hills, I am everlasting and unmoved;
I am like an ocean without shores.

I am not bound by the body,
as the clear sky is not bound by clouds;
whence then should the characters
of waking, dreaming, dreamlessness, belong to me?

The veil comes, and, verily, departs again;
it alone performs works and enjoys them.
It alone wastes away and dies,
while I stand like a mighty mountain,
forever unmoved.

Neither forth-going nor return belong to me,
whose form is ever one, without division.
He who is the one Self, without fissure or separation,
perfect like the ether – how can he strive or act?

How should righteousness or sin belong to me,
who possess not the powers of sense, who am above emotion,
above form and change, who experience ever partless bliss;
for the scripture teaches that in the Self
is neither righteousness nor sin.

What is touched by his shadow,
whether heat or cold, or foul or fair,
touches not at all the man,
who is other than his shadow.

The natures of things beheld touch not the beholder,
who is apart from them, sitting above unchanged,
as the character of the house affects not the lamp.

Like the sun which witnesses the act,
like the tongued flame that leads the conflagration,
like the rope that holds what is raised;
thus am I, standing on the summit, the conscious Self.

I am neither the actor, nor the causer of acts;
I am neither he who enjoys, nor he who brings enjoyment;
I am neither the seer, nor he who gives sight;
I am the unequalled Self, self-luminous.

When the disguise moves,
just as the foolish-minded attribute to the sun
the dancing of its reflection on the water,
so one thinks: I am the doer, the enjoyer; I, also, am slain.

Let this inert body move on the waters or on dry land;
I am not thereby stained by their natures,
as the ether is not stained by the nature of a jar.

Acting, enjoying, baseness or madness,
inertness or bondage or unloosing
are the changes of the mind,
and belong not really to the Self,
the supreme Eternal, the pure, the secondless.

Let Nature suffer changes ten times,
a hundred, a thousand times;
what have I to do with these commotions?
For the lowering clouds touch not the sky.

From the unmanifest, down to grossest things,
all this world encountered is a mere reflection only.
Like the ether, subtle, without beginning or end,
is the secondless Eternal; and what that is, I am.

All-embracing, illumining all things;
under all forms all-present, yet outside all;
everlasting, pure, unmoved, unchanging,
is the secondless Eternal; and what that is, I am.

Where the differences made by glamour
have sunk to final setting,
of hidden nature, perceived in secret,
the Real, Wisdom, Bliss, and formed of bliss,
is the secondless Eternal; and what that is, I am.

Without act am I,
without change, without division, without form;
without wavering am I, everlasting am I,
resting on naught else, and secondless.

I am altogether the Self, I am the All;
I transcend all; there is none but me.
I am pure, partless awakening;
I too am unbroken bliss.

This sovereignty, self-rule, and mighty power,
through the goodness of thy pity, power, and might,
has been gained by me, my guide, great-souled;
honor, honor to thee, and yet again honor.

In that great dream that glamour makes,
in that forest of birth and age and death,
I wandered wearying; daily stricken by the heat,
and haunted by the tiger of selfishness;
thou hast saved me, my guide, by waking me out of sleep.

THE PERFECT SAGE

(Verses 519 – 548)

THE PUPIL SPEAKS:

Honor to that one Being, wherever it is;
honor to the Light which shines through the form of all that is;
and to thee king of teachers!

Beholding him thus paying honor
– a pupil full of worth, full of the joy of soul-vision,
awakened to reality –
that king of instructors, rejoicing in his heart,
that mighty souled one, addressed to him this final word:

THE TEACHER SPEAKS:

This world is the offspring of the Eternal's thought;
thus, verily, the Eternal is the Real in all things.
Behold it thus by the vision of the higher Self,
with mind full of peace, in every mode of being.
A certain Being, apart from form, is seen everywhere,
by those who have eyes to see.

Therefore knowers of the Eternal understand
that whatever is other than this,
is but the sport and workmanship of the intellect.

Who, being wise,
and tasting that essence of supreme bliss,
would delight any more in things of emptiness?
Who desires to look on a painted moon,
when the moon, the giver of delight, is shining?

For through enjoyment of unreal things,
there is no contentment at all, nor any getting rid of pain.
Therefore contented by enjoying
the essence of secondless bliss,
stand thou rejoicing,
resting on the Self that is true being.

Therefore beholding thyself everywhere,
and considering thyself as secondless,
let the time go by for thee, mighty minded one,
rejoicing in the bliss that is thine own.

And wavering doubt in the Self of partless awakening
which wavers not, is but of fancy's building;
therefore through the Self which is formed of secondless bliss,
entering into lasting peace, adore in silence.

In the silence is the highest peace,
because wavering is the intellect's unreal work;
there the knowers of the Eternal, mighty-souled,
enjoy unbroken happiness of partless bliss,
recognizing the Self as the Eternal.

There is no higher cause of joy than silence
where no mind-pictures dwell;
it belongs to him who has understood the Self's own being;
who is full of the essence of the bliss of the Self.

Whether walking or standing, sitting or lying down,
or wherever he may be, let the sage dwell according to his will,
the wise man finding joy ever within himself.

No distinctions of place or time, position or space
are to be regarded as bringing release from bondage,
for the mighty-souled, who has perfectly attained to reality.
Of what avail are the rites of religion
for one who has attained to wisdom?

What religious rite will help one to know a jar,
without having perceived it?
But where there is direct perception,
the object is perfectly understood.

So when there is direct perception,
the Self shines forth clearly,
without regard to place or time or rites of purification.

The direct knowledge, that "I am Devadatta,"
depends on nothing else;
and it is precisely thus with the knowledge that
"I am the Eternal," in the case of the knower of the Eternal.

How could the not Self, the mere chaff of unreality,
be the illuminer of that through the radiance of which
the whole world shines, as through the sun?

How can the scriptures or laws or traditions,
or even all beings,
illumine that by which alone they gain their worth?

This Self, self-illumined, is of unending power,
immeasurable, the direct knowledge of all;
knowing this, the knower of the Eternal, freed from bondage,
most excellent, gains the victory.

Things of sense neither distress nor elate him
beyond measure, nor is he attached to, or repelled by them;
in the Self he ever joys, the Self is his rejoicing;
altogether contented by the essence of uninterrupted bliss.

As a child, who is free from hunger and bodily pain,
finds delight in play, so the wise man rejoices,
free from the sorrow of "I" and "mine."

His food is what is freely offered, eaten without anxiety
or sense of poverty; his drink is the pure water of the streams;
he moves where fancy leads him, unconstrained;
he sleeps by the river-bank, or in the wood;
for his vesture is one that grows not old or worn;
his home is space; his couch, the world;
he moves in paths where the beaten road is ended;
the wise man, delighting in the supreme Eternal.

Dwelling in this body
as a mere temporary halting-place,
he meets the things of sense just as they come,
like a child subject to another's will;
thus lives the knower of the Self,
who shows no outward sign,
nor is attached to external things.

Whether clothed in space alone, or wearing other
vestures, or clothed in skins, or in a vesture of thought;
like one in trance, or like a child, or like a shade,
he walks the earth.

Withdrawing desire from the things of desire,
ever contented in the Self,
the sage stands firm through the Self alone.

Now as a fool, now a wise man;
now as a great and wealthy king; now a wanderer, now a sage;
now dwelling like a serpent, solitary; now full of honor;
now rejected and unknown;
thus the sage walks, ever rejoicing in perfect bliss.

Though without wealth,
contented ever; ever rejoicing,
though without sensuous enjoyments;
though not like others, yet ever seeming as the rest.

Ever active, though acting not at all;
though tasting no experience, yet experiencing all;
bodiless, though possessing a body;
though limited, yet penetrating all.

This knower of the Eternal,
ever bodiless,
things pleasant or painful touch not at all,
nor things fair or foul.

For pleasure and pain, things fair and foul,
are for him who is bound by the vestures,
who believes them real;
but for him whose bonds are broken,
for the sage whose Self is real Being,
what fruit is fair, or what is foul?

Just as in an eclipse of the sun,
people say, "the sun is darkened,"
though the sun indeed is not darkened,
and they speak ignorantly,
knowing not the truth of things.

Thus verily they behold
the most excellent knower of Brahma
as though bound to a body,
while he is in truth freed for ever from the body,
and they are deluded by the mere seeming of the body.

FOR EVER FREE

(Verses 549 – 561)

THE SERPENT'S SLOUGH

But the body he has left,
like the cast-off slough of a snake, remains there,
moved hither and thither by every wind of life.

As a tree is carried down by a stream,
and stranded on every shallow;
so is his body carried along to one sensation after another.

Through the mind-pictures
built up by works already entered on,
the body of him who has reached freedom
wanders among sensations, like an animal;
but the adept himself dwells in silence, looking on,
like the center of a wheel, having neither doubts nor desires.

He no longer engages his powers in things of sense,
nor needs to disengage them;
for he stands in the character of observer only.
He no longer looks at all to the personal reward of his acts;
for his heart is full of exultation,
drunk with the abounding essence of bliss.

Leaving the path of things known or unknown,
he stands in the Self alone; like a god in presence
is this most excellent knower of the Eternal.

Though still in life, yet ever free; his last aim reached;
the most excellent knower of the Eternal,
when his disguise falls off, becoming the Eternal,
enters into the secondless Eternal.

Like a mimic,
who has worn the disguises of well being and ill,
the most excellent knower of the Eternal
was Brahma all the time, and no other.

The body of the sage who has become the Eternal
is consumed away, even before it has fallen to the ground –
like a fresh leaf withered – by the fire of consciousness.

The sage who stands in the Eternal, the Self of being,
ever full, of the secondless bliss of the Self,
has none of the hopes fitted to time and space
that make for the formation of a body of skin, and flesh,
subject to dissolution.

Putting off the body is not freedom,
anymore than putting away one's staff and waterpot;
but getting free from the knots of unwisdom in the heart –
that is Freedom, in very deed.

Whether its leaf falls in a running river,
or on holy ground, prepared for sacred rites,
what odds does it make to the tree for good or ill?

Like the loss of a leaf, or a flower, or a fruit,
is the loss of the body, or powers, or vital breath, or mind;
but the Self itself, ever one's own, formed of bliss,
is like the tree and stands.

The divine saying declares the Self
to be the assemblage of all consciousness; the real is the actor,
and they speak only of the destruction of the disguise –
unwisdom.

THE SELF ENDURES

(Verses 562 – 574)

Indestructible, verily, is the Self –
thus says the scripture of the Self,
declaring that it is not destroyed
when all its changing vestures are destroyed.

Stones, and trees, grass, and corn, and straw
are consumed by fire, but the earth itself remains the same.
So the body, powers, life, breath and mind
and all things visible, are burned up by the fire of wisdom,
leaving the being of the higher Self alone.

As the darkness, that is its opposite,
is melted away in the radiance of the sun,
so, indeed, all things visible are melted away in the Eternal.

As, when the jar is broken,
the space in it becomes clear space,
so, when the disguises melt away,
the Eternal stands as the Eternal and the Self.

As milk poured in milk, oil in oil, water in water,
becomes perfectly one,
so the sage who knows the Self becomes one with the Self.

Thus reaching bodiless purity,
mere Being, partless, the being of the Eternal,
the sage returns to this world no more.

He whose forms born of unwisdom are burnt up
by knowledge of oneness with the everlasting Self,
since he has become the Eternal,
how could he, being the Eternal, come to birth again?

Both bonds and the getting rid of them
are works of glamour, and exist not really in the Self;
they are like the presence of the imagined serpent
and its vanishing, in the rope which really does not change.

Binding and getting rid of bondage
have to be spoken of, because of the existence,
and yet the unreality, of enveloping by unwisdom.
But there is no enveloping of the Eternal; it is not enveloped
because nothing besides the Eternal exists to envelop it.

The binding and the getting rid of bondage
are both mirages;
the deluded attribute the work of thought to the thing itself;
just as they attribute the cloud-born cutting off of vision
to the sun; for the unchanging is secondless consciousness,
free from every clinging stain.

The belief that bondage of the Real, is,
and the belief that it has ceased,
are both mere things of thought;
not of the everlasting Real.

Therefore these two, glamour-built,
bondage and the getting rid of bonds, exist not in the Real;
the partless, changeless, peaceful; the unassailable, stainless;
for what building-up could there be in the secondless,
supreme reality, any more than in clear space?

There is no limiting, nor letting go,
no binding nor gaining of success;
there is neither the seeker of Freedom, nor the free;
this, verily, is the ultimate truth.

BENEDICTION

(Verses 575 – 580)

This secret of secrets supreme, the perfect attainment,
the perfection of the Self, has been shown to thee by me today;
making thee as my new-born child,
freed from the sin of the iron age,
all thought of desire gone, making towards Freedom.

Thus hearing the teacher's words
and paying him due reverence, he went forth,
free from his bondage, with the Master's consent.

And he, the Teacher,
his mind bathed in the happy streams of Being,
went forth to make the whole world clean, incessantly.

Thus, by this Discourse of Teacher and Pupil,
the character of the Self is taught to those seeking Freedom,
that they may be born to the joy of awakening.

Therefore let all those who put away and cast aside
every sin of thought, who are sated with this world's joys,
whose thoughts are full of peace,
who delight in words of wisdom,
who rule themselves,
who long to be free,
draw near to this teaching,
which is dedicated to them.

To those who, on the road of birth and death,
are sore stricken by the heat
that the rays of the sun of pain pour down;
who wander through this desert-world,
in weariness and longing for water;
this well-spring of wisdom, close at hand, is pointed out,
to bring them joy – the secondless Eternal.
This Teaching of Sankara's bringing Liberation,
wins the victory for them.

Thus is ended *The Crest-Jewel of Wisdom*,
made by the ever-blessed Sankara,
pupil at the holy feet of Govinda his Teacher,
the supreme Swan,
the Wanderer of the World.

THE AWAKENING TO THE SELF

(ATMA BODHA)

This awakening to the Self is recorded for those
whose inner darkness has been worn away by strong effort,
who has reached restfulness,
from whom passion has departed,
who seek perfect Freedom.

Among all causes,
wisdom is the only cause of perfect Freedom;
as cookery without fire,
so perfect freedom cannot be accomplished without wisdom.

Works cannot destroy unwisdom,
as these two are not contraries;
but wisdom destroys unwisdom,
as light the host of darkness.

At first wrapped in unwisdom,
when unwisdom is destroyed
the pure Self shines forth of itself,
like the radiant sun when the clouds have passed.

When life that was darkened by unwisdom
is made clear by the coming of wisdom,
unwisdom sinks away of itself,
as when water is cleared by astringent juice.

This world is like a dream,
crowded with loves and hates;
in its own time it shines like a reality;
but on awakening it becomes unreal.

This passing world shines as real,
like the silver imagined in a pearl-shell,
as long as the Eternal is not known,
the secondless substance of all.

In the real conscious Self,
the all-penetrating everlasting pervader,
all manifested things exist, as all bracelets exist in gold.

Just like the ether, the Lord of the senses,
the Radiant, clothed in many vestures,
seems divided because these are divided,
but is beheld as one when the vestures are destroyed.

Through this difference of vesture,
race, name, and home are attributed to the Self,
as difference of taste and color to pure water.

Built up of fivefold-mingled elements
through accumulated works is the physical vesture,
the place where pleasure and pain are tasted.

Holding the five life-breaths, mind, reason,
and the ten perceiving and acting powers,
formed of unmingled elements, is the subtle vesture,
the instrument of enjoyment.

Formed through the beginningless, ineffable error
of separateness, is the causal vesture.
One should hold the Self to be different
from these three vestures.

In the presence of the five veils,
the pure Self seems to share their nature;
like a crystal in the presence of blue tissues.

The pure Self within should be wisely discerned
from the veils that surround it,
as rice by winnowing, from husk and chaff.

Though ever all-present,
the Self is not everywhere clearly beheld;
let it shine forth in pure reason
like a reflection in a pure mirror.

The thought of difference arises through the vestures,
the powers, mind, reason, and nature;
but one must find the Self,
the witness of all this being,
the perpetual king.

Through the busy activity of the powers,
the Self seems busy;
as the moon seems to course through the coursing clouds.

The vestures, powers, mind, and reason
move in their paths under the pure consciousness of the Self,
as people move in the sunshine.

The qualities of vestures, powers, and works
are attributed to the spotless Self through undiscernment,
as blue to the pure sky.

Through unwisdom,
the mental vesture's actorship is attributed to the Self,
as the ripple of the waves to the moon reflected in a lake.

Passion, desire, pleasure and pain move the mind;
but when the mind rests in deep sleep they cease;
they belong to the mind, not to the Self.

Shining is the sun's nature;
coldness, the water's; heat, the fire's;
so the Self's nature is Being, Consciousness, Bliss,
perpetual spotlessness.

The Self lends Being and Consciousness,
and mind lends activity.
When these two factors are joined together by undiscernment,
there arises the feeling that 'I perceive.'

The Self never changes;
and mind of itself cannot perceive;
but the Self through error believes itself
to be the habitual doer and perceiver.

The Self is believed to be the habitual life,
as a rope is believed to be a snake; and thus fear arises.
But when it is known that 'I am not the habitual life
but the Self' then there can be no more fear.

The Self alone lights up the mind and powers,
as a flame lights up a jar.
The Self can never be lit by these dull powers.

In the knowledge of the Self,
there is no need that it should be known by anything else.
A light does not need another light; it shines of itself.

Putting all veils aside,
saying 'It is not this! It is not this!'
one must find the real unity of the habitual self
and the Supreme Self,
according to the words of wisdom.

All outward things,
the vestures and the rest, spring from unwisdom;
they are fugitive as bubbles.
One must find the changeless, spotless
'I am the Eternal.'

As I am other than these vestures,
not mine are their birth, weariness, suffering, dissolution.
I am not bound by sensuous objects,
for the Self is separate from the powers of sense.

As I am other than mind,
not mine are pain, rage, hate, and fear.
The Self is above the outward life and mind,
according to the words of wisdom.

From this Self comes forth the outward life and mind,
and all the powers;
from the Self comes ether, air, fire, the waters, and earth;
upholder of all.

Without quality or activity,
everlasting, free from doubt, stainless, changeless, formless,
ever free am I the spotless Self.

Like ether, outside and inside all, I am unmoved;
always all-equal, pure, unstained, spotless, unchanged.

The ever-pure lonely one,
the partless bliss, the secondless, truth, wisdom, endless,
the Supreme Eternal; this am I.

Thus the steadily-held remembrance that
'I am the Eternal' takes away all unwisdom,
as the healing essence stills all pain.

In solitude, passionless, with powers well-ruled,
let him be intent on the one, the Self,
with no thought but that endless one.

The wise through meditation
immersing all outward things in the Self,
should be intent on that only Self,
spotless as shining ether.

Setting aside name, color, form,
the insubstantial causes of separateness,
the knower of the supreme
rests in perfect Consciousness and Bliss.

The difference between knower, knowing, and known
exists not in the Self;
for through its own Consciousness and Bliss
it shines self-luminous.

Thus setting the fire-stick of thought
in the socket of the Self,
let the kindled flame of knowledge
burn away the fuel of unwisdom.

By knowledge, as by dawn,
the former darkness is driven away;
then is manifest the Self,
self-shining like the radiant sun.

Yet the Self, though eternally possessed,
is as though not possessed, through unwisdom.
When unwisdom disappears,
the Self shines forth like a jewel on one's own throat.

Separate life is conceived in the Eternal by error,
as a man is imagined in a post.
But the pain of separation ceases
when the truth about it is perceived.

By entering into real nature, wisdom swiftly arises.
Then the unwisdom of 'I' and 'mine' disappears, as when
a mistake about the position of north and south is set right.

The seeker after union, possessed of all knowledge,
sees with the eye of wisdom that all things rest in the Self;
and this Self is the One, the All.

Self is all this moving world; other than Self is naught.
As all jars are earth, so he beholds all as the Self.

Perfect Freedom even in this life is this, that a man
should shake himself free from all the limits of his disguises,
through the essence of Reality, Consciousness, Bliss,
just as the grub becomes the bee.

Crossing the ocean of glamour,
and slaying the monsters, passion and hate,
the seeker for union, perfect in peace,
grows luminous in the garden of the Self.

Free from bondage to outward, unlasting pleasures,
and returning to the joy of the Self,
he shines pure within like the flame in a lamp.

Even when hidden under disguises,
let the Sage stand free from them, like pure ether.
Though knowing all, let him be as though he knew nothing;
moving untrammeled like the air.

Let the Sage, shaking off his disguises,
merge himself utterly in the all-pervading One;
as water in water, ether in ether, flame in flame.

The gain above all gains, the joy above all joys,
the wisdom above all wisdoms;
let him affirm that it is the Eternal.

When this is seen, there is no more to see;
when this is attained, there is no more to attain;
when this is known, there is no more to know;
let him affirm that this is the Eternal.

Upward, downward, on all sides perfect;
Being, Consciousness, Bliss;
the secondless, endless, everlasting One;
let him affirm that this is the Eternal.

Through the knowledge that nothing is but the Eternal,
the unchanging One is beheld by the wise;
the aboriginal, partless joy;
let him affirm that this is the Eternal.

As partakers in the bliss of that partless, blissful One,
the Evolver and all the powers enjoy their bliss as dependents.

Every being is bound to the Eternal;
every movement follows the Eternal;
the all-embracing Eternal is in all,
as curd is in all milk.

Nor small nor great nor short nor long,
nor born nor departing, without form, attribute, color, name;
let him affirm that this is the Eternal.

Through whose shining shine the sun and all lights;
but who shines not by any's light;
through whom all this shines;
let him affirm that this is the Eternal.

All present within and without,
making luminous all this moving,
the Eternal shines forth glowing of red-hot iron.

The Eternal is different from the moving world –
yet other than the Eternal is naught!
What is other than the Eternal shines insubstantial,
like the mirage in the desert.

Things seen and heard are not other than the Eternal.
Knowledge of reality teaches that all this is the Eternal,
the being, Consciousness, Bliss, the secondless.

The eye of wisdom beholds
the ever-present Consciousness, Bliss, the Self,
the eye of unwisdom beholds not,
as the blind beholds not the shining sun.

The personal life,
refined through and through by the fire of wisdom,
which right learning and knowledge kindle,
shines pure as gold, freed from every stain.
The Self, rising in the firmament of the heart – sun of wisdom,
darkness-dispersing, all-present, all-supporting –
shines forth and illumines all.
He who, drawing away from space and time,
faithfully worships in the holy place of the divine Self – the
ever-present, the destroyer of heat and cold and every limit,
the stainless, eternally happy –
he all-knowing, entering the All, becomes immortal.

(Thus the Awakening to the Self is completed.)

THE AWAKENING TO REALITY

(TATTVA BODHA)

SANKARA'S CATECHISM

INTRODUCTORY BY CHARLES JOHNSTON

*In the "Awakening to the Self," and, still more, in the
"Crest Jewel of Wisdom," Sankara the Teacher uses many
words in a clear, precise, and consciously exact sense,
which is not always to be gathered from the context of these
two works. In the "Awakening to the Self," this is hardly an
impediment, as the expression of this excellent poem is so
perfect and universal; nor is there any great impediment in
the first part of the "Crest Jewel of Wisdom," which has been
translated under the title "First Steps on the Path."
But further on in the "Crest Jewel" itself these definitions are
not always to be found. What is to be done then,
if we really want to understand the Teacher precisely?*

*Happily Sankara has left us a Key in his own work,
the "Awakening to Reality," where nearly every special word
of his philosophy is exactly defined. We have only to try to
find the best English translation of his definitions,
and we shall have a clear clue and outline to the larger work,
the "Crest Jewel," and, indeed,
to the whole of Sankara's philosophy.*

*One thing must be remembered.
This "Awakening to Reality" is what we have called it –
a catechism. And in a catechism we can hardly expect the
perfect poetical form and splendid imagery of works like the
"Awakening to the Self." What we shall find, is lucidity,
accuracy, grasp, coherence; but not poetical beauty.*

THE AWAKENING TO REALITY

I

To the Master, the World-Soul,
the Master of seekers for union, obeisance;
to the teacher, the giver of wisdom.
To fulfill love for those who would be free,
this *Awakening to Reality* is addressed to them.

THE FOUR PERFECTIONS

We shall tell of the way of discerning reality,
the perfection of freedom,
for those who are fitted by possessing the Four Perfections.

What are the Four Perfections?

The discerning between lasting and unlasting things;
No Rage for enjoying the fruit of works, either here or there;
the Six Graces that follow Peace;
and then the Longing to be free.

What is the discerning
between lasting and unlasting things?

The one lasting thing is the Eternal;
all, apart from it, is unlasting.

What is No Rage?

A lack of longing for enjoyments here
and in the heaven-world.

What is possession of the Perfections that follow Peace?

Peace;
Self-Control;
Steadiness;
Sturdiness, Confidence;
Intentness.

What is Peace?

A firm hold on emotion.

What is Self-Control?

A firm hold on the lust of the eyes
and the outward powers.

What is steadiness?

A following out of one's own genius.

What is sturdiness?

A readiness to bear opposing forces,
like cold and heat, pleasure and pain.

What is confidence?

Confidence is a reliance on the Voice of the Teacher
and Final Wisdom.

What is Intentness?

One-pointedness of the imagination.

What is the Longing to be free?

It is the longing: "That Freedom may be mine."

THE DISCERNING OF REALITY

These are the Four Perfections.
Through these, men are fitted to discern Reality.

What is the Discerning of Reality?

It is this: the Self is real; other than it, all is fancy.

SELF, VESTURES, VEILS, MODES

What is the Self?

He who stands apart from the Physical, the Emotional,
and the Causal Vestures; who is beyond the five Veils;
who is witness of the three Modes;
whose own nature is Being, Consciousness, Bliss —
this is the Self.

THE THREE VESTURES

What is the Physical Vesture?

Being formed of the five creatures not fivefolded,
born through works, the perfection of the enjoyment
of opposing forces like pleasure and pain,
existing with its seventeen phases:
the five powers of knowing; the five powers of doing;
the five lives; emotion, one; the soul, one,
this is the Emotional Vesture.

The five powers of knowing are:
Hearing, Touch, Sight, Taste, Smell.
Hearing's radiation is Space; Touch's, Air; Sight's, the Sun;
Smell's the Twin Physicians; these are the powers of knowing.

Hearing's business is the seizing of sounds;
Touch's business, the seizing of contacts;
Sight's business, the seizing of forms;
Taste's business, the seizing of tastes;
Smell's business, the seizing of odors.

The five powers of doing are:
Voice, Hands, Feet, Putting-forth, Generating.
Voice's radiation is the Tongue of Flame; Hand's, the Master;
Feet's, the Pervader; Putting-forth's, Death;
Generating's, the Lord of Beings;
thus the radiations of the powers of doing.

Voice's business is speaking;
Hand's business is grasping things; Feet's business is going;
Putting-forth's business is removing waste;
Generating's business is physical enjoying.

What is the Causal Vesture?

Being formed through
ineffable, beginningless unwisdom,
it is the Substance and Cause of the two Vestures;
though unknowing as to its own nature,
it is yet in nature unerring; this is the Causal Vesture.

THE THREE MODES

What are the Three Modes?

The Modes of Waking, Dreaming, Dreamlessness.

What is the Mode, Waking?

It is where knowledge comes through Hearing
and the other knowing powers,
whose business is sound and the other perceptions;
this is the Waking Mode.

When attributing itself to the Physical Vesture,
the Self is called the Pervading.

Then what is the Mode, Dreaming?

The world that presents itself in rest,
generated by impressions
of what has been seen and heard in the Mode, Waking,
is the Mode, Dreaming.

When attributing itself to the Emotional Vesture,
the Self is called the Radiant.

What then is the Mode, Dreamlessness?

The sense that I perceive outwardly nothing at all,
that rest is joyfully enjoyed by me,
this is the Mode, Dreamlessness.

When attributing itself to the Causal Vesture,
the Self is called the Intuitional.

THE FIVE VEILS

What are the Five Veils?

The Food-formed; the Life-formed;
the Emotion-formed; the Knowledge-formed;
the Bliss-formed.

What is the Food-formed?

Coming into being through the essence of food,
getting its growth through the essence of food,
in the food-formed world it is again dispersed,
this is the Food-formed Veil – the Physical Vesture.

What is the Life-formed?

The Forward-life and the four other Lives,
Voice and the four other powers of doing;
these are the Life-formed.

What is the Emotion-formed Veil?

Emotion, joining itself to the five powers of knowing –
this is the Emotion-formed Veil.

What is the Knowledge-formed?

The Soul, joining itself to the five powers of knowing –
this is the Knowledge-formed Veil.

What is the Bliss-formed?

This verily is the Substance not quite pure because of the unwisdom that gives birth to the Causal Vesture; in it are founded all joys; this is the Bliss-formed Veil.

Thus the Five Veils.

By saying: "Mine are the lives; mine is emotion; mine is the soul; mine is the wisdom"; these are recognized as possessions. And just as a bracelet, a necklace, a house and such things separated from one's self, are recognized as possessions, so the Five Veils and the Vestures, recognized as possessions, are not the Self.

What then, is the Self?

It is that whose own-nature is Being, Consciousness, Bliss.

What is Being?

What stands through the Three Times (*Present, Past, Future*) – this is Being.

What is Consciousness?

The own-nature of Perceiving.

What is Bliss?

The own-nature of Joy.

Thus let a man know that the own-nature of his own Self is Being, Consciousness, Bliss.

EXPLANATORY BY CHARLES JOHNSTON

*This "Awakening to Reality" is a summary of an
intuition of the world, a solution of the universe.
Only those who have certain mental and moral endowments
are ripe for the understanding of such a solution of the world.
Briefly, these endowments are: wisdom and will.
The solution reached is –
the real Self of every man is the Eternal.
This Self is inwardly beginningless, endless, immortal.
But outwardly it becomes manifest as three lesser selves,
each with its own vesture, its own world.*

*Lowest of these is the physical self, the "Pervading";
with its physical Vesture, in the Waking world.*

*Next, the emotional self, the "Radiant,"
with its emotional Vesture, in the Dreaming world.*

*Highest, the causal self, the "Intuitional,"
with its causal Vesture, in the Dreamless world.
It has existence apart from the Eternal,
owing only to the thin veil of illusion, which hides the identity
of the One with the All. Thus, as to its own nature,
it is unknowing; for, while believing itself One, it is really All.
But for all other things it is unerring, for its close proximity
to, and real oneness with, the Eternal, give it the inner sense
of the trueness of things that is all wisdom.
This is "the Seer who ordained all fitly through the ages."*

*In the Physical Vesture adheres the one Veil;
in the Emotional Vesture three –
the vital, the emotional, the moral;
in the Causal, again one.*

*There is great difficulty in finding a fit word for the
term we have translated "radiation." What is meant is the
power – personified, almost personal – conceived to be the
"regent" or "deity" of the field in which each mode of
perception and action finds its expansion.*

A closely analogous phrase would be, for instance,
"the Prince of the Powers of the Air," who would thus be the
"regent" or "deity" of the powers of touch, and, in morals,
the "lusts of the flesh."

This is, of course, mythology:
a mythical representation of an actual truth,
very difficult to represent otherwise than mythologically.

But in the conclusion of the matter there is no
difficulty. It is, that a man shall know the own-nature
of his own Self to be Being, Consciousness, Bliss;
or, in other words, Eternal, Wisdom, Love.

II

We shall speak now of the way
the four-and-twenty natures are developed.

THE PRIMITIVE SEVEN

Dwelling together with the Evolver in glamour,
who is the very self of the three potencies:
substance, force, and space.

From this glamour, shining ether came forth.

From shining ether, breath came forth.

From breath, fire came forth.

From fire, the waters came forth.

From the waters, earth came forth.

THEIR SUBSTANTIAL PARTS

Now, among these five natures:

From the substantial part of shining ether,
the power of hearing came forth.

From the substantial part of breath,
the power of touch came forth.

From the substantial part of fire,
the power of seeing came forth.

From the substantial part of the waters,
the power of taste came forth.

From the substantial part of earth,
the power of smelling came forth.

From the united substantial parts of these five natures,
the inner powers – mind, soul, self-assertion, imagination –
came forth.

Mind is the very self of intending and doubting.

Soul is the very self of affirmation.

Self-assertion is the very self of attributing selfhood.

Imagination is the very self of image-making.

The regent of mind is the Moon.

The regent of soul is the Evolver.

The regent of self-assertion is the Transformer.

The regent of imagination is the Pervader.

THEIR FORCEFUL PARTS

Now, among these five natures:

From the forceful part of shining ether,
the power of voice came forth.

From the forceful part of breath,
the power of handling came forth.

From the forceful part of fire,
the power of moving came forth.

From the forceful part of the waters,
the power of engendering came forth.

From the forceful part of earth,
the power of extruding came forth.

From the united forceful parts of these natures,
the five lives – the upward life, the forward-life, the uniting-
life, the distributing-life, the downward-life – came forth.

THEIR SPATIAL PARTS

Of these five natures, from their spatial parts,
the five-folded elements come forth.

What is this five-folding?

It is this: taking the spatial parts of the five primitive
natures – one part of each – these parts are each first divided
in two; then one half of each part is left alone, on one side,
while the other halves of each are divided into four.
Then to the half of each nature, is joined the fourth of the half
of each of the other natures. And thus five-folding is made.

From these five primitive natures, thus five-folded,
the physical vesture is formed.
Hence the essential unity between the clod
and the Evolving Egg.

106

THE LIFE AND THE LORD

There is an image of the Eternal,
which attributes itself to the vestures, and is called the Life.
And this Life, through the power of Nature,
regards the Lord as separate from itself.

When wearing the disguise of Unwisdom,
the Self is called the Life.

When wearing the disguise of Glamour,
the Self is called the Lord.

Thus, through the difference of their disguises, there is
an appearance of difference between the Life and the Lord.
And as long as this appearance of difference continues,
so long will the revolving world of birth and death continue.
For this reason the idea of the difference between
the Life and the Lord is not to be admitted.

But how can the idea of unity between
the self-assertive, little-knowing Life,
and the selfless, all-knowing Lord, be accepted,
according to the famous words, *that thou art*;
since the genius of these two, the Life and the Lord,
is so opposite?

This is not really so;
for 'Life attributing itself to the physical
and emotional vestures' is only the verbal meaning of *thou*;
while the real meaning of *thou* is 'pure Consciousness,
bare of all disguises, in dreamless life.'

And so 'the Lord full of omniscience and power'
is but the verbal meaning of *that*;
while the real meaning of *that* is
'pure Consciousness stripped of disguises.'

Thus there is no contradiction in the unity
of the Life and the Lord,
since both are pure Consciousness.

THE FREE-IN-LIFE

And thus all beings in whom
the idea of the eternal has been developed,
through the words of wisdom and the true Teacher,
are Free-in-life.

Who is free in Life?

Just as there is the firm belief that 'I am the body,'
'I am a man,' 'I am a priest,' 'I am a serf,'
so he who possesses the firm conviction that
'I am neither priest nor serf nor man,
but stainless Being, Consciousness, Bliss,
the Shining, the inner Master, Shining Wisdom,'
and knows this by direct perception, he is Free-in-life.

THE THREE MODES OF DEEDS

Thus by the direct knowledge that 'I am the Eternal,'
he is freed from all the bonds of his deeds.

How many modes of these 'deeds' are there?
If counted as 'deeds to come,' 'deeds accumulated,'
and 'deeds entered on,' there are three modes.

The pure and impure deeds
that are done by the body of the wise, after wisdom is won,
are called 'deeds to come.'

And what of 'deeds accumulated'?
The deeds that are waiting to be done,
sprung from seeds sown in endless myriads of births,
are 'deeds accumulated.'

And what are 'deeds entered on'?
The deeds that give joy and sorrow here in the world,
in this vesture, are 'deeds entered on.'
Through experiencing them they reach cessation;
for the using-up of deeds entered on comes through
experiencing them.

And 'deeds accumulated' reach cessation through wisdom,
the very self of certainty that 'I am the Eternal.'
'Deeds to come' also reach cessation through wisdom.
For, as water is not bound to the lotus-leaf,
so 'deeds to come' are not bound to the wise.
For those who praise and love and honor the wise,
to them come the pure 'deeds to come' of the wise.
And those who blame and hate and attack the wise,
to them come all the unspeakable deeds,
whose very self is impurity,
of the wise man's 'deeds to come.'

THE END

Then the Knower of the Self,
crossing over the circling world,
even here enjoys the bliss of the Eternal.
As the sacred books say:
The Knower of the Self crosses over sorrow.
And the sacred traditions say:
Whether he leaves his mortal form in Benares
or in a dog-keeper's hut,
if he has gained wisdom, he is free,
his limitations laid aside.

Thus the Awakening to Reality is completed.

SANKARA'S CATECHISM

EXPLANATORY BY CHARLES JOHNSTON

*In the first part of Sankara's Catechism, previously
translated, the most valuable thing is the teaching of the
sevenfold man, who is really a modified unity appearing in
seven modes. The only real and eternal element in the
sevenfold man – for real and eternal are, for Sankara,
synonymous terms – is the perfect Self, which is one with the
Eternal. In manifestation this Self appears in three degrees:
the intuitional self, the emotional self, the physical self;
and, for each of these there is a vesture suited to its nature.
Thus the divine Self, with its three degrees,
and their three vestures, make up the perfect seven.*

*The three lesser degrees of the Self are its
representatives in the three manifest worlds:
the spiritual world, the middle world, the physical world.
And, very naturally, the middle world partakes in some
degree of the nature of the other two; so that its highest layer
is touched with the nature of the spiritual world, while its
lowest layer is touched with the nature of the physical world.*

*This threefold nature of the middle world finds its
counterpart in the three veils which make up the vesture of
the middle self, which we have called the emotional self
as perhaps the best description of its total nature.*

*The three veils of the middle self are the vital veil,
the sensuous veil, and the intellectual veil; and the regents of
the last two are 'mind' and 'soul,' as we have translated the
original terms – Manas and Buddhi.*

*Development takes place, therefore, by the gradually
raising of the self through these vestures and veils; so that,
having begun as the physical self in pure animal life,
it gradually becomes the emotional and intellectual self of
human life, then the intuitional self of life that is something
more than human, and at last realizes itself as the eternal
Self which is one with the Eternal.*

To this, the first part of the Catechism, is then added the outline of Sankara's idealistic physics, the doctrine of the three potencies of substance, force, space; or, as one might call it, from a different point of view, the three modes of subject, predicate, object: of the knower, the knowing, the known. And as perception is of five types, the subject, predicate, and object are divided into the five types of sensuous perception. But as the objects of sensuous perception are not simple, but each responds to several different sensations, a description is found for this fact in the 'process of five-folding' of the object. As an example, a piece of camphor responds not only to the sense of sight but to other senses, touch, taste, smell; it is therefore conceived as made up of the five natures that are objects of sensuous perception, so mingled that one nature is dominant. The three potencies and the five natures are the three vestures and the five veils, from another point of view. Very important are the definitions: 'mind' is the power of intending and doubting; 'soul' is the power of affirmation; the latter approaching the intuitional self which is the 'enlightened spiritual will.' To express in terms of morals this psychological analysis, we may say that at first through the power of self-assertion, the idea of selfhood is falsely attributed to the physical body and its animal nature, and then to the mental picture of the physical body, which is the emotional self or lower personality. The task of regeneration, of initiating true life, consists in first checking this false self-assertion – selfishness and sensuality – and then through the stages of 'intending and doubting' and strong 'affirmation' substituting for the lower personality the enlightened spiritual will, which is the direct expression of the real Self, re-becoming the Eternal. Then this chapter of physics and psychology is followed by one of metaphysics.
There is the real Self, which is the Eternal.
But we do not realize our life as that real Self.
Why do we not realize it? Because of two errors, or illusions, which make up the double 'heresy of separateness.'
The first error is the error of our apartness from the Eternal.
The second error is the error of our apartness from each other.

111

The removal of these two errors constitutes 'our duty
towards God' and 'our duty towards our neighbor'; in both
cases the real gain is our own, is the gain of our real Self.
Sankara calls the first error glamour; the second, unwisdom.
The picture of the self formed through the first is the Lord;
the picture of the self formed through the second is the Life.
And the real nature of both is the same — pure consciousness
— though there is a verbal difference,
a difference of definition, between them.
Then, in conclusion, the three forms of 'deeds' or Karma.
We may compare 'accumulated deeds' to capital;
'deeds entered on,' to interest; and 'deeds to come,'
to the earnings of an unselfish man for the good of others.
And we must remember that each of these has a debit
as well as a credit side. The real value of this little treatise is
as a key and outline of longer and more complicated works;
yet it has a high excellence of its own.

THE ESSENCE OF THE TEACHING

(VAKYA SUDHA OR BALA BODHANI)

SEER AND SEEN

The form is the seen, the eye is the seer;
the mind is both the seen and the seer.
The changing moods of the mind are the seen,
but the witnessing Self, the seer, is never seen.

The eye, remaining one, beholds various forms;
as, blue and yellow, coarse and fine, short and long;
and differences such as these.

The mind, remaining one, forms definite intentions,
even while the character of the eye varies,
as in blindness, dullness, or keen-sightedness;
and this holds also of hearing and touch.

The conscious Self, remaining one,
shines on all the moods of the mind:
on desire, determination, doubt, faith, unfaith,
firmness and the lack of it, shame, insight, fear,
and such as these.

This conscious Self rises not, nor has its setting,
nor does it come to wax or wane;
unhelped, it shines itself, and illumines others also.

THE PERSONAL IDEA

This illumining comes
when the ray of consciousness enters the thinking mind;
and the thinking mind itself is of twofold nature.
The one part of it is the personal idea;
the other part is mental action.

The ray of consciousness and the personal idea
are blended together, like the heat and the hot iron ball.
As the personal idea identifies itself with the body,
it brings that also a sense of consciousness.

The personal idea is blended with the ray of
consciousness, the body, and the witnessing Self, respectively
– through the action of innate necessity, of works,
and of delusion.

Since the two are bound up together,
the innate blending of the personal idea
with the ray of consciousness never ceases;
but its blending with the body ceases,
when the works wear out;
and with the witnessing Self, through illumination.

When the personal idea melts away in deep sleep,
the body also loses its sense of consciousness.
The personal idea is only half expanded in dream,
while in waking it is complete.

The power of mental action,
when the ray of consciousness has entered into union with it,
builds up mind-images in the dream-state;
and external objects, in the waking state.

The personal form, thus brought into being by
the personal idea and mental action, is of itself quite lifeless.
It appears in the three modes of consciousness;
it is born, and so also dies.

THE POWERS OF GLAMOUR

For the world-glamour has two powers –
extension and limitation, or enveloping.
The power of extension
brings into manifestation the whole world,
from the personal form to the universal cosmos.

This manifesting is
an attributing of name and form to the Reality –
which is Being, Consciousness, Bliss, the Eternal;
it is like foam on the water.

The inner division between the seer and the seen,
and the outer division between the Eternal and the world,
are concealed by the other power, limitation;
and this also is the cause of the cycle of birth and death.

The light of the witnessing Self
is united with the personal form;
from this entering in of the ray of consciousness
arises the habitual life – the ordinary self.

The isolated existence of the ordinary self
is attributed to the witnessing Self, and appears to belong to it;
but when the power of limitation is destroyed,
and the difference appears,
the sense of isolation in the Self vanishes away.

It is the same power which conceals
the difference between the Eternal and the visible world;
and, by its power, the Eternal appears subject to change.

But when this power of limitation is destroyed,
the difference between the Eternal and the visible world
becomes clear; change belongs to the visible world,
and by no means to the Eternal.

The five elements of existence are these:
being, shining, enjoying, form and name;
the three first belong to the nature of the Eternal;
the last two, to the nature of the visible world.

In the elements – ether, air, fire, water, earth;
in creatures – gods, animals, and men,
Being, Consciousness, Bliss are undivided;
the division is only of name and form.

Therefore setting aside this division
through name and form,
and concentrating himself on Being, Consciousness, Bliss,
which are undivided,
let him follow after soul-vision perpetually,
first inwardly in the heart,
and then in outward things also.

Soul-vision is either fluctuating or unwavering;
this is its two-fold division in the heart.
Fluctuating soul-vision is again two-fold;
it may consist either in things seen or heard.

This is the fluctuating soul-vision
which consists in things seen:
a meditating on consciousness as being merely the witness
of the desires and passions that fill the mind.

This is the fluctuating soul-vision
which consists in things heard:
the constant thought that "I am the Self, which is unattached,
Being, Consciousness, Bliss, Self-shining, secondless."

The forgetting of all images and words,
through entering into the bliss of direct experience –
this is unwavering soul-vision,
like a lamp set in a windless place.

Then, corresponding to the first,
there is the soul-vision which strips off name and form
from the element of pure Being, in everything whatever;
now accomplished outwardly, as it was before, in the heart.

And, corresponding to the second
is the soul-vision which consists in the unbroken thought,
that the Real is a single undivided Essence,
whose character is Being, Consciousness, Bliss.

Corresponding to the former third,
is that steady being, is the tasting of this Essence for oneself.
Let him fill the time by following out these,
the six stages of soul-vision.

When the false conceit, that the body is the Self,
falls away; when the Self supreme is known;
then, whithersoever the mind is directed,
there will the powers of soul-vision arise.

The knot of the heart is loosed; all doubts are cut;
all bondage to works wither away –
when That is known, which is the first and the last.

THE THREE SELVES

The individual self appears in three degrees:
as a limitation of the Self; as a ray of the conscious Self;
and, thirdly, as the self imagined in dreams.
The first alone is real.

For the limitation in the individual self
is a mere imagination;
and that which is supposed to be limited is the Reality.
The idea of isolation in the individual self is only an error;
but its identity with the Eternal is its real nature.

And that song they sang of "That thou art"
is for the first of these three selves alone;
it only is one with the perfect Eternal, not the other selves.

The power of world-glamour, existing in the Eternal,
has two potencies: extension and limitation.
Through the power of limitation,
Glamour hides the undivided nature of the Eternal, and so
builds up the images of the individual self and the world.

The individual self which comes into being
when the ray of consciousness enters the thinking mind,
is the self that gains experience and performs works.

The whole world, with all its elements and beings,
is the object of its experience.

These two, the individual self and its world,
were before time began;
they last till freedom comes, making up our habitual life.
Hence they are called the habitual self and world.

In this ray of consciousness, the dream-power exists,
with its two potencies of extension and limitation.
Through the power of limitation it hides the former self
and world, and so builds up a new self and a new world.

As this new self and world
are real only so long as their appearance lasts,
they are called the imaginary self and the imaginary world.
For, when one has awakened from the dream,
the dream existence never comes back again.

The imaginary self
believes its imaginary world to be real;
but the habitual self knows that world to be only mythical,
as also is the imaginary self.

The habitual self looks on its habitual world as real; but
the real Self knows that the habitual world is only mythical,
as also is the habitual self.

The real Self knows its real oneness with the Eternal;
it sees nothing but the Eternal,
yet sees that what seemed the unreal is also the Self.

As the sweetness, the flowing, and the coldness,
that are the characteristics of the water, reappear in the wave,
and so in the foam that crests the wave:

So, verily,
the Being, Consciousness, and Bliss of the witnessing Self
enter into the habitual self that is bound up with it;
and, by the door of the habitual self,
enter into the imaginary self also.

But when the foam melts away,
its flowing, sweetness, coldness, all sink back into the wave;
and when the wave itself comes to rest,
they sink back to the sea.

When the imaginary self melts away,
its Being, Consciousness, Bliss sink back into the habitual self;
and, when the habitual self comes to rest,
they return to the Self supreme, the witness of all.

THE TEACHINGS OF SANKARA

BY CHARLES JOHNSTON

*Tradition, our best guide in many of the dark
problems of India's past, attributes the admirable
philosophical work we have just translated to
Sankaracharya, the greatest name in the history of Indian
Philosophy, and one of the greatest masters of pure thought
the world has ever seen.*

*Sankara, again according to the tradition of the East,
lived and taught some two thousand years ago, founding
three colleges of Sanskrit learning and philosophy,
the most important being at Sringeri, in southern India.
He wrote Commentaries on the older Vedanta books,
and many original works of great excellence,
of which this is reckoned to be one.*

*Like all of Sankara's separate works,
"The Essence of the Teaching" is complete in itself,
containing a survey of the whole of life,
from a single standpoint;
in the present case, from the point of view of pure intellect.*

*The moral problem before us, is the liberation of our
souls from the idea of personality; and the opening of the
door to the life of the universal Self, which will enter our
hearts, and rule them, once the personal idea is put out of the
way. And there is no more potent weapon for combating the
personal idea than the clear and lucid understanding that
what we call our personality is, in reality, only one of many
pictures in the mind, a picture of the body, held before our
consciousness, viewed by it, and therefore external to it.
If the personality is a picture in the field of consciousness,
it cannot be consciousness itself; cannot be our real self;
but must necessarily be unreal and transient.*

*We are the ray of consciousness, and not the image of
the body which it lights up, and which, thus lit up,
we call our personality.*

120

And here we come to one point of the highest interest, in the present work: its central ideas anticipate, almost in the same words, the most original teachings of German philosophy. Hence a right understanding of it will bridge over one of the chasms between the East and the West, the remote past and the life of today; thus showing, once more, that the mind of man is everywhere the same; that there is but one Soul making itself manifest throughout all history.

It may be enough, here, to point out that German philosophy – the teaching of Kant, as developed by Schopenhauer – regards each individual as a manifestation of the universal Will, a ray of that Will, fallen into manifestation, under the influence of the tendency called the will-towards-life.

This individualized ray of the universal Will, falling into the intellect, becomes thereby subject to the powers which make for manifestation, and which Kant analyzed as Causality, Time, and Space. For Kant has shown, with admirable cogency and lucidity, that these so solid-seeming realities are not real at all, but were forms of our thought; mere figments of our intellects. What we call manifestation, Schopenhauer calls representation; and he has very fully developed the idea of the Universe as the resultant of the universal Will, manifested through these three forms of representation – Causality, Time, and Space.

Now it is quite clear that he calls Universal Will what Sankara, following the Upanishads, calls the Eternal; and that the forms of representation of Schopenhauer's system, correspond to the World-glamour, or Maya, of Indian thought. And it is further clear that the will-toward-life, or desire for sensuous existence, of the one system, is very close to the personal idea, or egotism, of the other.

Whoever is acquainted with the two systems,
can point out a further series of analogies;
we shall content ourselves with alluding to one.
Schopenhauer taught that our salvation lies in denying the
personal and selfish will-toward-life, within ourselves,
and allowing the Universal Will to supersede it;
the very teaching which lies at the heart of Indian thought:
the supersession of the individual self by the Self universal,
the Self of all beings.

To turn now from the purely intellectual,
to the moral side of the matter: if we consider it well, and
watch the working of the powers of life we find within us,
we shall see that all our misery and futility
come from this very source, the personal idea –
the vanity and selfishness of our own personalities,
coming into strife with the equally vain and selfish
personalities of others.

There is not an evil that cannot be traced to this fertile
source. Sensuality, for example, with all its attendant crime
and pain, is built on two forces, both springing from the
personal idea: first, the desire for the stimulus of strong
sensation, to keep the sense of the separate, isolated self
keen and vivid; and then the vanity and foolish admiration of
our personal selves, as possessors of such abundant means of
gratification. Another evil, the lust of possessions,
is of the same brood; and, curiously enough, the root of it is –
fear; the cowering fear of the personal self,
before the menacing forces of the world; the desperate, and –
infallible accompaniment of cowardice – remorselessly cruel
determination to build up a triple rampart of possessions
between the personality and the mutability of things.
The whole cause of the race for wealth, the cursed hunger for
gold, is a fearful and poltroon longing for security,
protection for the personal self; which, indeed,
as a mere web of dreams and fancies,
is in very bad need of protection.

*The last evil, ambition, which is only vanity grown up,
is so manifestly of the same color with the others that no
special indication of the fact is needed. Thus we see what an
immense part of human life, and that, the most futile and
pitiable part of it, is built up on so slight a foundation:
the wholly mythical personality, the web of dreams, the mere
image of a body, itself unreal, which has usurped a sort of
sovereignty over all the powers of our wills and minds.*

*The whole problem for us is this,
and it is one that recurs in every moment of life:
to disperse this web of dreams which we call our personality,
and so to let the pure and universal Will pour into our hearts,
to follow out its own excellent purposes, and manifest its own
beneficent powers. And thus we shall for the first time enter
into our inheritance; no longer as shadowy and malevolent
sprites, raging between earth and heaven,
a sorrow to the angels, a mockery to the fiends;
but rather as undivided parts of the great soul of humanity;
of that universal Self, whose own nature is
perfect Being, perfect Consciousness, perfect Bliss.*

THE SONG OF THE SELF

(SIDDHANTA-TATTVA-VINDU)

Nor earth nor water, fire nor liquid, air nor ether,
nor the powers, nor these in one;
undifferentiated, in dreamless perfect rest,
That, the One, final, blest, alone, am I.

Nor castes nor their divisions, rite nor rule, are mine,
nor fixing mind and thought and mood;
no longer dreaming things not Self art 'I' and 'mine,'
That, the One, final, blest alone, am I.

Nor mother, father, nor gods and worlds,
nor scriptures, offerings, shrines are there, they say,
in dreamlessness abandoned by the lonely Self;
That, the One, final, blest, alone, am I.

Nor sectary of Cause or Lord or Life knows That,
nor follower of Saint or Rite,
in perfect union, pure of all but the Self,
That, the One, final, blest, alone, am I.

Nor upward, downward, nor within, without;
nor midward, backward, That, nor east nor west;
all-present everywhere in partless unity,
That, the One, final, blest, alone, am I.

Nor white nor black nor yellow, That, nor red;
nor small nor very great nor short nor long;
formless, yet like a light, a star;
That, the One, final, blest, alone, am I.

Nor teacher, teaching, learner, what is learned;
nor thou nor I nor this expanded world;
conscious of its own form, from error free,
That, the One, final, blest, alone, am I.

Even expanded for the sake of Self
— Self, that, still perfect, on no other rests —
all the wise world besides is little worth.
That, the One, final, blest, alone, am I.

Nor is this first with any second to it;
nor lonely this, nor yet has it compeers;
nor is this secondless One void or filled with aught;
how shall I tell this perfect wisdom's crowd?

Please use the contact form at seeseer.com to let us know if reading the Crest Jewel of Wisdom and Other Writings of Sankaracharya was a good experience for you.

Other books published by The Freedom Religion Press that you may be interested in are:

1. The Seven Steps to Awakening is a collection of quotes by Ramana Maharshi, Nisargadatta Maharaj, Sankara, Vasistha, Muruganar, Sadhu Om and Annamalai Swami.

2. Powerful Quotes from Sankara.

3. Three Hundred Quotes from Hinduism from more than forty sources.

4. Developing Spiritual Consciousness Second Abridged Edition by Swami Mukerji.

5. The Crest Jewel of Discrimination by Sankara translated by John Richards.

For information about these and other spiritual books go to:

www.seeseer.com

Made in the USA
Monee, IL
15 April 2020